AF326641

Praise for *The Akashic Way*

Most of us hear the whisper of inner wisdom from time to time. It's been thrilling to witness Mary Madeiras—Emmy Award-winning director—lean into that wisdom more and more over the years, and now let it lead her. This book shows the reader how. And how sweet it is.

—ELSIE MAIO, CEO, mentor, and founder,
The SoulBranding™ System

Mary Madeiras offers a luminous masterclass in soul alignment. *The Akashic Way* is a sacred tuning fork for leaders, creators, and visionaries seeking to build in harmony with higher truth. If you intend to shape this world with authenticity and impact, begin here.

—BRENT N. HUNTER, author of *The New Game* and
The Rainbow Bridge: Bridge to Inner Peace and to World Peace

The Akashic Way is an inspiring, beautifully written, and deeply illuminating book. Mary Madeiras shares her personal path with authenticity, vulnerability, and wisdom. Her insights are grounded, accessible, and profoundly transformative, opening a gateway to an inner knowing on a soul level. This book is a must-read for anyone curious about connecting with the deeper truths of their existence.

—REV. DR. TEMPLE HAYES, global thought leader,
author of *When Did You Die* and *Being a Difference Maker*

Imagine glimpsing our world from the Akashic Records—seeing how universal truths change the very essence of who we are and how we live here on Earth. Mary Madeiras offers us this revelation. *The Akashic Way* shows us how to move from fear and separation to love—the deep goodness that dwells within us This book is a rare and precious gift.

—FLO MAGDALENA, author of *I Remember Union: The Story of Mary Magdalena* and *Sunlight on Water: A Guide to Soul-full Living*

I could feel timelines collapsing as the Divine spoke through Mary, weaving past and future into a single, eternal moment. This book is a living transmission. Each chapter carries the vibration of unity, reminding us that nothing is ever lost . . . calling us to remember the wholeness we already are.

—DOYLE BRAMHALL II, guitarist, producer, and songwriter

The Akashic Way offers timeless wisdom and truth, arriving at a moment of great challenge and awakening. Mary Madeiras shares the extraordinary gift of the Akashic Records, reminding us that "we are one and we are not alone." Her words serve as both blueprint and guide, offering support from the Akashic Realm for a new way of living and being in alignment.

—CHRISTINA JONES, executive spiritual director of The Althea Center, professional speaker, teacher, and coach

The Akashic Way is filled with pearls of wisdom—a direct transmission from the soul of the Universe to the heart of the reader. Mary Madeiras has cracked open the door; all you have to do is step through, sink into the words, and take a ride. What begins as Mary's ride will slowly become your ride into fuller understanding and full acceptance of life. I invite you to join in this magical mystery ride.

—DR. NINA MEYERHOF, EdD, sacred activist and founder, Children of the Earth, co-founder, One Humanity Institute

The greatest love story ever written! Reignite your soul's sparkle! This conversation with Mary Madeiras and the Akashic Records brings to life the cosmic dance of the physical world and the Divine spirit already within you. Mary's real-life dialogue with the Akashic Records is very personal and simultaneously conveys an important message to humanity. During these most turbulent and unsettling times, this book provides you with practical messages of hope, joy, and most of all, LOVE!

—REV. DR. HEATHER SHEA, animal intuitive, author, mystic

Mary Madeiras invites us to be open and curious about the sensory perceptions of the seen and unseen. Through dynamic dialogues with the light energies of the Akashic Records, she bravely shares her own trials and the wisdom they revealed. Whether you are a novice or advanced on your spiritual path, each chapter offers practical guidance for self-development and the tools to formulate a universal self-mastery plan.

—DENISE McDERMOTT, MD

The Akashic Way is a spiritual companion that reminds us we are never alone in our search for answers. Mary Madeiras interprets the Divine with eloquence and authenticity, making the experience feel like an intimate conversation with a wise, loving friend. Her voice will leave a lasting imprint on your heart. This book is a powerful tool for anyone on a spiritual journey.

—TAMMY LEECH, executive producer, media consultant

Every page felt like a mirror, gently reflecting me back to myself. It reminded me that healing isn't about fixing what's broken—it's about remembering what's already whole and that I am already complete. This is a beautiful guide for anyone on the path of truth, spiritual curiosity, and Divine love.

—KAMELA BREWER, president, Inner Gold Collective

What makes this book remarkable is its accessibility. You can read it cover to cover, or simply open to any chapter and find the exact insight you need in that moment—one of those rare books that meets you where you are. I found myself completely engrossed by the wisdom within and by the thoughtful, intuitive way Mary structured each chapter.

—MARLA GOLDBERRG, Doctor of Metaphysics and Healing,
author, co-founder/Global Consciousness Summit

The Akashic Way is an invitation to return to one's wholeness and connection to the source of all things, which is love. In clear and very personal language, Mary Madeiras opens us to experience the wisdom of the Akashic field of energy, knowledge, intuition, and universal compassion that resides in each of us, and to be fully "awakened" in service to all beings on Earth and the Universe. Receiving its wisdom is a timeless blessing.

—MICHAEL FITZPATRICK, cellist, composer,
and cultural peace leader

The Akashic Way is an extraordinary blend of memoir and sacred revelation, offering profound guidance for those seeking a deeper understanding of spiritual truth. Through her unique access to the Akashic Records, Mary delivers powerful Divine messages that inspire reflection, healing, and enlightenment. It's a treasure trove of wisdom that will resonate deeply with anyone longing to connect with the sacred mysteries of life.

—JACK R. BIALIK, author of *Lost in Time: Our Forgotten*
and *Vanishing Knowledge*

The Akashic Way

THE AKASHIC WAY

Living Through the Lens of the Akashic Records

Mary Madeiras

PRECOCITY PRESS

Editor: Joyce Walker
Creative Director and Book Design: Susan Shankin
Cover Design: Sonia Horne
Cover Art: *Blue Moon and Empty Arms* by Lee Passarella
Precocity Press, Los Angeles, CA

ISBN: 978-1-972561-05-8 (hardcover)
ISBN: 979-8-9931150-9-2 (paperback)
ISBN: 979-8-9931150-4-7 (ebook)

Library of Congress Control Number: 2025920273
First edition printed in the United States of America

To my family—whose struggles, sorrows, anger, and judgment became my unlikely teachers. Through the immense pain and sadness that I witnessed and experienced, I found my voice—a voice that whispered *Their path is not your path.* Had I not endured such aching sadness, I may never have longed so fiercely to live a life of balance, love, and beauty—a life where kindness rules.

To my teachers, the Ursuline nuns—the gentle souls who raised me in light and, unknowingly, held me in the darkness of my childhood, and who, through word and presence, taught me that God's love lives within. Their devotion to peace and community became the compass I have carried through every season of my life.

To my wife, Christine—my luminous, wild-hearted force of nature—whose fierce love of this planet and courageous vision for a new Earth inspire me daily. She recognized a power in me long before I claimed it for myself. She is my mirror, my muse, my home, and my love.

CONTENTS

PREFACE

THE STORY OF HOW I came to the Akashic Records was not instant or obvious. It unfolded over time—through a series of events that, at first, felt like career detours and personal disappointments, but in hindsight, were clear signs guiding me toward something deeper.

I had spent years building a successful career as a television director. I worked at the CBS, NBC, and ABC networks in news and sports as well as on seven network daytime dramas, including *General Hospital*. By the time I was working on *General Hospital*, I had earned two Emmy Awards and a Directors Guild of America Award. I was thriving. Then one day, my contract with *General Hospital* was not renewed. There was no explanation, and the news came as a shock—not only to me, but also to the actors and crew I had been working with and had grown close to. I felt lost and confused. What made it even more surreal was that I had received an Emmy Award nomination for the work I had done before my departure. I ended up winning the Emmy and accepted the award on live television at Radio City Music Hall—all while no longer being part of the show. It was bittersweet.

What followed was a kind of forced introspection. I started questioning whether the career I had poured myself into for decades was truly my calling or if those years had been wasted. I sought answers wherever I could. I leaned into spiritual exploration, attending numerous workshops with Abraham-Hicks and exploring the teachings of Eckhart Tolle, Dr. Bruce Lipton, Gregg

Braden, Dr. Joe Dispenza, and many others. Still, something was missing. I continued to interview for directing work, even though it appeared that this chapter of my life was over. I now know that I had lost touch with my soul's chosen purpose—and the Akashic Records guided me back to it.

One day, I was having a psychic reading in Huntington Beach, California. I had been seeing this psychic regularly, and on this particular day, she told me that she was "seeing" a man over my right shoulder. I was intrigued by who he could be. She said he was my protector, had been with me forever, and that he "translates sacred geometry into ideas that are then given to me." What is so interesting is that often I would be working on a scene with an actor or group of actors, and I would suggest a unique way to play a scene, and one of the actors would respond, "I love that idea. Where did you get it?" I would unknowingly wave my right hand above me and out to the right and say, "It wasn't me. It just came in." That day, when the psychic mentioned my protector, I wanted to know more. She said, "He protects your Akashic Records." I asked her what the Akashic Records were, and she said she didn't know. I went home that day and looked them up on the Internet. Something about this resonated deeply for me, but I didn't act on it right away.

Then I received another sign. During a visit to my favorite metaphysical bookstore in Los Angeles, while alone in a back room, my attention was drawn to a book sticking out oddly from a shelf above me. I pulled it down and stared at the title—*How to Read the Akashic Records* by Linda Howe. I knew this was meant for me. I bought the book and read it in one sitting. It felt less like I was learning something new and more like I was remembering something I had always known. I began opening my Akashic Records and experienced a flow of thought and insight that was unlike anything I had ever known—and it was effortless. The love I felt in those readings was profound and unmistakably Divine.

The third sign came on my birthday, when my dear friend gifted me the opportunity to formally study with Linda Howe at her Center for Akashic Studies. That was it—I enrolled and earned two certifications, the latter an advanced practitioner certification.

During my studies, when I opened my Akashic Records, the messages that came through were so profound that they helped me move through blocks and subconscious programs I hadn't realized were running my life. Soon after, I began opening the Akashic Records of my friends. The results were amazing!

I still wondered, though, why I had worked for so many years in a career that might not have been fully aligned with my soul's path. I brought this question to my Akashic Records, and the response was both clear and transformative. My Records helped me uncover subconscious patterns that had blocked my ability to see my light, my power, and most of all, my creativity. In that reading, my Records encouraged me to access a part of myself I believed I could never be: a writer.

Since childhood, I had been attracted to anything connected to imagination and storytelling, so the talent for writing was somewhere inside me—yet I was afraid of it and filled with self-doubt. What I learned in my readings was that I had chosen television directing because it allowed me to be *close* to storytelling without taking the full risk of owning my voice as a writer, and that I was afraid that if I stepped into my true creative purpose, I might have nothing left to reach for. The Records reassured me that writing would not end me—it would begin me. This Akashic exchange marked a turning point in my life.

I have come to learn, through my work in the Akashic Records, that nothing is ever a mistake—ever.

In a later exchange, I was reminded of a subconscious program that was running in the background of my mind—a belief that certain people are destined for greatness and that I was not one of them. I discovered that this was an ancestral program. I grew up in an Irish-Portuguese working-class family, and my parents and siblings didn't realize their own potential greatness. It wasn't their fault; it was simply how they, their parents, and their grandparents were raised. Once I discovered this through my work in the Akashic Records, things began to change for me.

Another insight that emerged from that Akashic exchange was this thought: *What if I completed what I came to do in this lifetime? Then what? Do I die?* I had never consciously thought about that. I imagine how successful creatives may burden themselves with this idea. What happens after they paint their greatest masterpiece, write the Pulitzer Prize-winning novel, or win an Oscar? Is it over? Having those thoughts or beliefs can block the creative flow. The Akashic Records have lots to say about this topic in this book.

Trauma was another block I processed through my Akashic Records journey. Whether rooted in past lives or childhood, trauma is a common theme that many of my clients bring into their sessions. When we view trauma through the lens of our Akashic Records, we are able to transform it into an opportunity. In my experience, this is what sets the Records apart from so many other healing modalities.

Everything is energy, and energy never dies. While working in the Akashic Records, we are shown by our Divine entourage—the keepers of our Akashic Records—how to glean the energy of trauma and bring that energy (not the trauma itself) into our present lives, where it returns to the light and love that we are, empowering us to become the whole, complete, unique individuals we have chosen as our destiny.

Every soul enters this world with a purpose—a Divine alignment that is never lost, only forgotten. The Akashic Records serve as a mirror, reflecting our path back to us. There are no mistakes, only choices, each guiding us toward deeper understanding, growth, and ultimate happiness.

INTRODUCTION

A KASHA IS A SANSKRIT word meaning primary substance—that from which all things are born. The concept of the Akashic Records is that there exists a quantum Divine Realm that began as a blank slate upon which we, as souls, imprint our experiences, thoughts, actions, and the information related to our soul's chosen roles across our lifetimes. When we open and visit our Akashic Records, we are able to access this information.

Edgar Cayce, known as the "sleeping prophet," was accessing the Akashic Realm throughout his work as a medical medium and healer.

This is an excerpt from the book *Edgar Cayce on the Akashic Records:*

> *The Akashic Records contain the history of every soul since the dawn of creation. These records connect each one of us to one another. They contain the stimulus for every archetypal symbol or mythic story which has ever deeply touched patterns of human behavior and experience. They have been the inspiration for dreams and invention. They draw us toward or repel us from one another. They mold and shape levels of human consciousness. They are a portion of Divine Mind. They are the unbiased judge and jury that attempt to guide, educate, and transform every individual to become the very best that*

she or he can be. They embody an ever-changing fluid array of possible futures that are called into potential as we interact and learn from the data that has already been accumulated.

The Edgar Cayce readings suggest that each of us writes the story of our lives through our thoughts, our deeds, and our interactions with the rest of creation. This information has an effect upon us in the here and now. In fact, the Akashic Records have such an impact upon our lives and the potentials and probabilities we draw toward us that any exploration of them cannot help but provide us with insights into the nature of ourselves and our relationship to the Universe.[1]

At the beginning of my Akashic journey, most of my readings centered around my personal issues, blocks, and concerns. But as my time in the Records increased, I experienced additional insights—downloads of profound thoughts, ideas, and suggestions—for humanity. It became clear to me that I had to share these Divine messages.

The material in this book is a combination of excerpts from my personal readings plus specific topics for humanity that were lovingly suggested by the Divine Akashic entourage.

Regardless of how we perceive this material, a healing activation occurs each time we reread or listen back to the messages. As the Masters, Teachers, and Loved Ones of the Akashic Records often remind us—when we revisit these exchanges, they literally change, offering a new and more appropriate understanding of ourselves and our ultimate healing. It is both amazing and profound—something I cannot logically explain. We benefit from the Akashic Records no matter when, where, or how we revisit them. They are timeless.

---

[1] Kevin J. Todeschi, *Edgar Cayce on the Akashic Records* (A.R.E. Press, 1998), xii.

Through my vast experience working in the Akashic Records, I have come to know them as a powerful Divine tool for life. The Records reside inside each of us all the time.

There is no structure or format to *The Akashic Way*. I tried to wrestle it into a progression of ideas and themes, searching for a perceived flow to the material, but it was impossible! I finally surrendered to what I have personally learned from my time in the Records—where there is Divine, there is never a formula. There is no beginning, middle, or end.

The spark of creation lives within each of us, and every moment of our lives is part of a greater choreography we chose before incarnating. Understanding this allows us to step onto our highest path with trust and grace.

I promise that for whatever you are seeking in your life—at any moment—if you bring it into your consciousness, hold this book in your hands, and open *The Akashic Way* to any page, you will receive something wonderful that will "trigger" you back to YOU.

I am honored to share my journey to and through the Akashic Records.

Pretty amazing stuff, my friends.

WHAT PEOPLE WANT TO KNOW

I'VE BEEN INTERVIEWED numerous times over the years on podcasts and radio shows and asked to speak about the Akashic Records and describe my role in helping people recognize their Divine power as shown through their Records. What follows are frequently asked questions and my responses that I hope will bring clarity about the Akashic Records and ignite a personal recognition of your own inner Divine light.

Some think of the Akashic Records as tangible books or manuscripts. Is it this vast book library somewhere?

The Akashic Records are not a physical place but a Divine space—not an actual library. Because we are speaking esoterically, our logical brains may ask, "Well, what is it? Where is it? Can I touch it?" Well, no. It is a realm, and it has existed since the beginning of humanity. The term *Akashic Records* emerged in the 1800s, popularized by figures like Madame Blavatsky, founder of the Theosophical Society. Renowned medical medium and psychic Edgar Cayce—known as the "sleeping prophet"—accessed the Akashic Realm.

The Akashic Records exist inside us. As Jesus taught, God—or Source—is not outside of us; it lies within us. When we open our Records, we access the Divine aspect of ourselves. We speak to the light essences of our soul's recorded history, including our present experiences. So no, it is not a literal library. However, that's a great word for it, because, like a library, it is where we can discover and remember anything and everything about ourselves and our soul's chosen journey.

✳ *Where did the idea for the Akashic Records come from?*

My understanding is they have been around since the beginning of time. Throughout humanity's history, it was primarily mystics and holy people who accessed the Akashic Records. As time has advanced, humanity, the planet, and consciousness have expanded, and the veil has become thinner, making it easier to hear beyond our third-dimensional reality.

✳ *Are the Akashic Records available to everyone?*

Yes, they are. Anyone can access their Akashic Records. Many religions have their own versions of the Akashic Records—for example, the Book of Life from the Bible. The idea of a Divine Realm that records not only our experiences but also who we are as souls has existed throughout history. Where did the idea begin? My answer is God. It began as Source itself.

✳ *What are the light energies you access in your Akashic Records work?*

I communicate with an entourage of light beings or energies who impart information and wisdom to my clients through me. This information mirrors each client's higher self and their soul's chosen journey.

The *Lords* of the Akashic Records are a collective consciousness responsible for the integrity and protection of the Records. The *Lords* maintain the sanctity of the Akashic Realm. They do not communicate directly with us but oversee access to the Records on a soul level.

Next in the entourage are the *Masters, Teachers, and Loved Ones,* who are the primary sources of guidance during an Akashic Records reading.

The *Masters* are light energies who have never been human. They offer guidance that is aligned with each soul's chosen journey.

The *Teachers* have also never lived human lives, but they work closely with us to help us learn and expand. They guide specific themes or lessons that occur throughout a lifetime. For example, if a person discovers through their Akashic Records that they incarnated into this lifetime to learn self-love, a teacher energy will help guide them as they experience self-love.

The *Loved Ones* are souls who have been human and with whom we have experienced love in this lifetime. It may be a mother who has transitioned, a teacher, or a dear friend. The *Loved Ones* maintain the integrity of our Akashic Records. They stand steadfast in the choice or reason we are on this planet at this time and offer us clarity from their Divine perspective.

At times during a client's Akashic Records reading, I will sense the presence of a *Loved One*, whose energy will, in turn, be recognized by my client as a familiar essence in their heart.

❋ *How do you experience a client's Akashic Records? What happens in your process?*

I begin a reading with a sacred prayer, using my client's legal name. During this prayer, I begin to receive blocks of thought that are not mine. It is very subtle—like slipping into an altered space—and I am both there and here at the same time. It is pure positive love. That is how I know I am in the Records.

I find it interesting that I don't have any personal interpretations during a reading. The sacred prayer, along with my intention and commitment to serving others in the name of the Divine, assists me in setting aside my ego. I simply allow the information to flow through me. The Divine moves on the spoken word, so as my clients express their needs or desires during the reading, I hear messages for them that provide clarity for what they are seeking.

✳ *Are there any requirements for accessing one's Akashic Records?*

In my experience, what is necessary to successfully open one's Akashic Records is an understanding, commitment, and desire to have an ongoing relationship with the essence of Divine—God, Source, Creator, the Universe—whatever you choose to call it.

I came to the Akashic Records without knowing anything about them—at least I thought I didn't know. But in time, I realized that deep down, I have maintained a profound connection to this Divine Realm since childhood. I was brought up Catholic and have a clear memory of sitting in church as a child and experiencing a beautiful energy—knowing that it was both outside of me and inside of me at the same time. I experienced this energy loving me.

Later in life, I discovered that what I had been experiencing was not the Catholic Church's teachings but rather—as Jesus taught—the God within me and around me. My connection—my knowing that there is a Source, a mastermind, an essence of love that has choreographed our grand humanity—began at an early age.

As an adult, when I first visited my Akashic Records, I experienced a *deep knowing* and discovered—or remembered—that I had a past life that made sense of it all for me.

✳ *What about becoming a practitioner? What is required?*

Besides having a connection to Source or God, I believe it is essential for practitioners to identify their own past traumas and wounds—whether from this lifetime, past lifetimes, or both—and allow them to transmute into useful assets in their lives. A huge part of my work when I was studying to become a practitioner involved healing my own wounds through my Akashic Records. Through my Akashic journey, I have learned and experienced that our past wounds—specifically the energetic imprint they carry—hold immense value and can play a key role in manifesting our soul's chosen journey in this lifetime, ultimately leading to greater peace, joy, and happiness.

Another key part of my ongoing ability to access the Akashic Records of others is my love for people. Since I was young, I never understood judgment or hatred. I grew up with a father who expressed anger and hatred toward other cultures, which never made sense to me. I love people, and I was often ridiculed for believing that people are inherently good. I *know* that every person on this planet of love *is* good. Everything is love, and Divine is love, so knowing and experiencing this truth deep inside me makes my journey with people into their Akashic Records a beautiful and easy process.

※ *Are the Akashic Records fixed or dynamic?*

Both. The part of the Akashic Records that is fixed relates to each soul's original identity. A soul chooses to incarnate at a specific time as part of a broad, overarching theme or purpose. That part is fixed. However, souls do not preselect the specific human experiences they will have. The dynamic part of the Akashic Records lies in how we choose to express or attain our soul's original reason for incarnating. For example, some souls may choose to enter into a chaotic planetary lifetime to participate in—or serve—the creation of world peace. That choice is fixed. But they will have unending choices in how they manifest world peace.

We do not tumble randomly onto the planet—it is a powerful choice.

Why, we may ask, do we keep coming back? It may be that the soul reincarnates continually until it reaches full alignment with its original purpose in joining humanity.

We might ask, then, what happens when we reach full alignment with the very first choice we made? The answer: We return to Source and can choose another purpose, incarnating again with a whole new set of choices that align with our newly chosen purpose.

Does it ever end? No, not according to the Akashic Realm.

✳ *How can one experience healing through their Akashic Records?*

The Akashic Records do not force change or magically solve our problems. What they offer is something deeper: clarity, affirmation, alignment, and ultimately, self-empowerment.

During an Akashic reading, the light of the Divine Realm moves through the reading. The energy is very subtle. It is a beautiful experience to be bathed with the light of our own Divine essence while in our Records. It is a love that we often do not experience in our daily lives. It is the love of God.

The Akashic entourage of energies encourages questions—through me—for the client, and as they answer those questions, a deeper remembering begins to unfold. As the reading progresses, that remembering transforms into clarity, understanding, and personal healing.

In addition, when we listen back to our recorded readings, the quantum energy within each session is still present. However, it shifts—morphing into exactly what we need to hear at that particular moment. This is because quantum energy never dies; it is not fixed. It moves and responds. So when we revisit a reading later, it may sound entirely different. That's because it is.

I've had clients tell me—even a year after their session—that when they relisten to their readings, the information feels new to them. That's because the quantum Divine energy aligns with where they are in their life at that time.

I have revisited my own Akashic readings from as far back as seventeen years ago, and the messages still meet me exactly where I am.

✳ *Does every living thing have its own Akashic Record?*

Yes. Back to the definition of Akasha: that from which all things are formed—a field that began as a blank slate. From the beginning of time, all thoughts, experiences, and actions of every living being have been imprinted into the Akashic Records—lifetime after lifetime. The trees, the animals, the ground beneath us, the rocks, the mountains, the air—everything—has its own Divine "voice" recorded in the Akashic Records.

When I work with pets, it's important that I have their permission. The way I work with them is simply to be in their presence and ask, "Can I open your Records?" I have done this with my own dogs and cats. They will convey their answer through their body language. They will look away or walk away if they don't want their Akashic Records to be opened. But if they stay engaged, that is a clear sign that they are giving their permission to open their Records. It is important to honor their wishes.

✳ *Can you open the Akashic Records of locations or places?*

Everything that exists in the public domain has its own Akashic Record—sacred spaces, places, specific addresses, even corporations.

Regarding corporations: The original essence of every company exists in the Akashic Realm. This essence finds its vibrational match in the form of its founder or CEO—a match to what it is and why it is here on the planet at this time. It may be a specific person or group who receives the idea and forms the company. It is a magnificent co-creation with that original essence.

Author Elizabeth Gilbert, in her book *Big Magic*, explains the creative process by sharing her theory about how creations are born, i.e., inventions, writings, paintings. She believes creativity originates as essence, floating in the ethers, looking for its vibrational match so that it may become manifest. My example of this is the essence of the story *Harry Potter,* which may have floated about looking for a way to become manifest. J. K. Rowling became that match.

When I open the Akashic Records of a corporation for its CEO or founder, who may be seeking clarity about the company's direction, I experience the essence of the company from its Masters, Teachers, and Loved Ones, who reflect that essence in the form of knowledge, information, and insight. The CEO, as its co-creator, receives clarity and affirmation to then realign with the company's original purpose. This renewed clarity often encourages the corporation's next steps and actions, which can lead to expansion, increased value, and ultimate success.

* *What do the Akashic Records tell us about God, the Divine, or Source?*

What I have known my entire life—and what has been affirmed for me from the Akashic Records—is that we *are* Source. It is Divine essence. It is love. What is God, we may ask? What I understand from the deepest part of me is that God is the essence of love itself. It exists now, always has, and always will. It is this love that sparked the creation of the Universe. And we *are* it. I invite you to feel the grandness of this—the grandness that each one of us is. The Divine Realm has affirmed for me that we are never separate from this.

* *What role do past lives and subconscious patterns play in the Akashic Records?*

Throughout my years working as a practitioner, I have encountered recurring themes that clients seek clarity on, such as "I feel lost and don't know where I'm supposed to be," "Why do I keep manifesting negative people?" "Why am I unhappy?" "Why am I sick all the time?" "Why am I stuck?" or "What is my life's purpose?" These were many of the same questions I had when I first began my journey into the Akashic Records.

Often, these concerns stem from experiences and unresolved energies from past lifetimes, which can confuse and hinder our growth and expansion in this lifetime. Science has shown that DNA is energy and that energy never dies—it simply shifts and changes. Therefore, past-life energies remain encoded in our DNA, accessible in the present—which means we have the ability to access them in the now. For example, if someone is dealing with a serious illness in their present life and discovers during an Akashic reading that they once lived a lifetime free of illness, that energetic imprint still exists. Through intention, they can reconnect with and activate that past-life imprint or memory—and in doing so, shift their present reality to one of "no illness."

Likewise, unexplained patterns, such as repeated relationship struggles or persistent dissatisfaction, can often be traced to past-life dynamics still at play. Clients who seem to "have it all" in this lifetime yet still feel inexplicably blocked often discover that what they are carrying did not begin in this lifetime. The Akashic Records illuminate these patterns, bathing them in Divine light and transforming them into tools for growth.

That said, not all blocks come from past lives. Many arise from subconscious patterns rooted in childhood. As Dr. Bruce Lipton teaches, these early subconscious programs can limit us long after they were formed. The Akashic Records support this view and take it further: Once a pattern is identified, we can access the energy beneath it and transmute it. What once held us back becomes an asset—or fuel—for forward movement.

CONVERSATIONS
WITH THE DIVINE

Now it's time to share messages from the Divine Realm that I've received through my Akashic readings. These sessions often began with questions about my own life, but what emerged was wisdom that is both universal and illuminating.

In the sections that follow, you will see that I used two identifiers to guide the flow of the dialogue:

AR: represents messages received from the Akashic Records.
M: indicates my thoughts, reflections, or questions.

This format will allow you to witness the unfolding conversation between my soul and the Divine Realm just as it happened.

A Note About the Transmissions

The messages from the Divine Realm, what I call transmissions, are presented exactly as I received them during my time in the Akashic Records. I did not edit their structure, grammar, or capitalization. Certain words may appear emphasized or styled in unique ways, and the phrasing may at times flow differently than conventional writing. They are presented here as given, as they hold unique energetic significance. I chose to honor the purity of the messages as they came through without filtering or reshaping them. They were received in a sacred space of alignment.

Let the rhythm and voice of these transmissions wash over you.

FEEL THE LOVE INSIDE YOU

WHEN I ASKED my Akashic Records what message should begin this book—one that would convey the greatest beauty for humanity—the answer came instantly, and with overwhelming beauty. It was love—the Divine love that *is* God/Source and that lives within each of us. This was the message that opened the door to everything that followed, and it remains one of the most sacred messages I have received.

AR: Beautiful. We shall begin. All beings on your Earth are infused with Divine love at their centers. This love is what generates life—before, now, and forever. Humans have become somewhat separated from their love centers, and when this happens, there forms a space through which the ego can grow. So, there then becomes three parts of a person: the person as they identify themselves, i.e., their looks, personalities, ideas, desires, etc.; the ego center, which bases its existence on lack of love; and the love center. The love we speak of is the pure, positive, Divine essence of all life—on your entire planet. It is where there are no perceptions, no perspectives, no judgments, no fear, no ego thoughts. Your planet is showing you this every day. Just look at your plant life, the air you breathe, the planet under your feet, the trees, the animal kingdom. They live in no judgment, no ego. They survive and thrive on the Divine law of love.

We are often asked by people in readings about how to remove blockages, how one can be happy, or how one can experience relief from pain or sadness. The answer is the same no matter what the issue: it is through the love of oneself.

How can humans experience this internal Divine love? The path will vary from person to person, but the journey remains the same.

Take some quiet time for you . . . it does not need to be meditation, but private you time. Look at your life and everything that has made you happy. Write these experiences down. Consider the things in your life that move you so much that you cease to think when you are near them, touch them, witness them, or watch them. Even if it brings you to tears, this is evidence of the Divine love that you hold inside. For example, if your heart breaks when you witness people hurting others or torturing animals, you may experience this as pain. However, pain is an ego perception that is not real. We are not invalidating the feelings you have in these moments, but when you experience what you refer to as immense pain or sadness, this is you experiencing the love you hold inside. And when these deep emotions emerge, whether positive or negative (again, your perceptions), you engage your heart at the exact moment of the experience. Here, you are at the quantum center point of all existence, where there is nothing and everything all at once. However, what can often happen immediately after these initial moments is that your mind and ego may step in to interpret it. It is then that it becomes what you call right, wrong, positive, negative, or horrible—and once your ego manufactures these thoughts, it can power them up into fear or anger. These can become the blockages you often ask about.

Consider how easy it can be to recognize what moves you—from the tiny bumblebee, to welcoming a newborn into the world, to seeing a child taking her first step, or watching a flower or an animal in its natural environment. These are just a few of the purest moments in life. How wonderful!

These are the mirror of the love you hold inside, without which you would never be able to recognize this magnificence to begin with.

We promise you that when you reimagine these joyful events, your life will soar. You will come to know yourself as love, and as this happens, your ego will relax its grip on you. We will speak on the ego later as its (perceived) influence is immense in your world today.

We encourage you to take a minimum of five minutes each day to engage in this Divine writing we are speaking of. Notice what takes your breath away—whether it is a moment of awe, honoring, laughter, surprise, shock, and even sadness. They all lead to one place: your heart. Your heart is showing you the love you hold inside. Feel it, bask in it, let it flow through the rest of your being, your body, mind, and soul. This is the magnificent you! Return to your Divine writings and reread them often. They will always meet you in the present moment and you will experience the love we speak of. This is not journaling. Journaling involves thoughts that flow from your mind to the page. We are suggesting Divine power-writing. Before long, your life will soar into everything you have ever hoped for.

Remember that every event in your life was chosen by you—on a deep soul level. And why would you do that? Because you are love and you deserve love, on every level. By re-experiencing this love, you feed back into the expansion of love itself on a much grander scale. This is Divine co-creation!

When my Masters, Teachers, and Loved Ones first conveyed this message, it deeply resonated with me. I began to take notice of the things in my life that move me. For me, it is animals, music, and the outdoors. I also love people—I love loving people. When I do, I experience something that reflects back to me, something I was never able to describe before. I now know—it's the love I have inside.

YOU ARE A HEALER

I WAS EXPERIENCING confusion—about both my diet and where I was living. My wife, Christine, was already on her journey to becoming vegan, and I was far from it. As so many of us have experienced, it can be challenging when our loved ones are nudging us toward their own exciting discoveries, and we are not quite there yet. It can feel like pressure if we're not ready to accept it or if it is simply not the right choice for us. I took my struggle into my Akashic Records. As a reminder, our Akashic Records are who we are. They mirror to us one hundred percent of the time what our soul's chosen role is in this lifetime. So, in essence, we get a healthy dose of ourselves! This was my reading.

M: First, my health. I am not feeling well. What is happening?

AR: Absolutely nothing to alarm yourself over. You are transitioning since the move from California. If you begin to have thoughts that you are well-suited to where you are living, it will all clear up, we assure you. You are in conflict over living in New York City. Until you resolve this inside of you, your body will keep telling you it is not happy either. Your body will follow your thoughts. We suggest that you proceed with what you have begun today. Get out and walk the city. Look around and take it all in. See and notice all the things that are special about New York. You will see your body begin to "take shape" as you do this. We recommend you do this privately, just for YOU.

M: Okay. I will do this. Do I need to see a doctor?

AR: If you do not, you will be fine. If you do, you will get more assistance as you work through this phase of your life. Your choice.

M: My diet—I still feel that there is something not quite right about the way I'm eating. I'm not in sync with how Christine eats, and I feel unhappy.

AR: Yes. Not a good thing for you. You must identify what foods work for you, Mary. Begin to experiment. You are already noticing the difference between whether your body is asking for you to eat something or your mind is tricking you into wanting something. Stop when this happens and take a few moments to listen to which one it is. It matters not what you eat, but what matters is what you think and feel about what you eat. You are beginning to express distress and anger over food and, therefore, blaming Christine. She is not the problem. How you handle your choices is the problem. You must feel good about what you eat. Yes, there are many foods in your world today that can be harmful to you. But you have the mechanisms in your bodies to handle anything. Your bodies have the intelligence and knowledge to transform anything into anything. You simply must practice this—try it a little at a time. There is no one food that is best for you humans. It is all good, and all has its place and role in your world. Just be comfortable about your food. When you are happy inside, you will only want the types of food that have happy energy. When you are feeling low or down on yourself, you will attract down and low-self-worth foods, or foods that contain that kind of energy. So, we want you to get out every day. Walk,

Mary... and listen to music a lot. It will bring your energetic field up into an arena of light and from that perspective, make your food choices. It is only then and under those conditions that the food will taste, feel, and be the right food for you. And it does not matter what all the books are saying. If you agree with them, then that is what will work for you, and you will be happy and healthy. Also, drink more water. You need this. But rest assured that you are okay. This is a minor hiccup in your life. We feel you feeling balanced. Yes?

M: Actually, yes, so balanced, I have no more questions. However, I know I came into this reading with many concerns. Where are they?

AR: Those concerns were coming from your ego, and you are not in that energetic field right now. The energy of ego cannot exist in the Akashic field. It will not work.

M: Should I continue to work in the Akashic Records and receive certifications as a practitioner?

AR: Your Records do show you as a teacher and a healer, Mary. You have been resisting this for some time now. You think it is the area you live in and the food you are eating or not eating that is causing your physical issues. It is not any of that. Feel how hot you are getting right now? This is your spiritual verifier. Listen carefully, Mary. Your Records show you are a healer. The more you step into this reality, the happier you will be, the better you will look, and the better you will physically feel. Study the Akashic Records. Embrace your role that you, yourself, chose. This lifetime for you is one of assisting others on how to gently move into their hearts and souls and away from ego and fear. You will benefit from these studies, and it will take you on your own in-depth journey back to a remembering of your Divine you. It will be a magnificent journey, we promise.

You will come to know yourself as light, and you will learn how to transform past traumas and confusions into the light. This is what will make you so valuable to others. You will become a steward of clarity and love. Your Akashic certifications will help others feel more comfortable taking the journey through you to their own Akashic Records.

I experience an immediate realignment each time I reread this Akashic exchange. Right after this reading, I raised my vibration through exercise, shifted my mindset around food and my body, and found myself naturally choosing healthy foods that made me happy. I made the choice to study to become an advanced Akashic Records practitioner, and through this journey, I discovered past lives and wounds that I transmuted into opportunities that are still manifesting today. Through my ongoing relationship with my inner Divine, my perception of my life has shifted to one of ease, grace, and joy.

I would like to remind you, dear reader, that you, too, are a lightworker. We are all Divine light and all connected in this way.

ALIGNING WITH
THE PATH ALREADY CHOSEN

I'VE BEEN WORKING in the Akashic Records for almost two decades, and each time I visit them, I learn more about humanity and the role we play in the bigger picture of planet Earth and the cosmos.

I chose the following Akashic exchange because it depicts how I begin my questions in my Akashic Records as specific and personal and how they often end in profound messages from the Divine for all of humanity.

I'm amazed at how timeless these messages are. This one, from approximately ten years ago, still resonates today. The quantum, ever-changing Divine is omnipresent.

M: Why do I feel so stuck in my next career moves?

AR: There is so much happening on your planet and beyond. Many of you are barely hanging on through the massive changes that are occurring. This is what you are experiencing. You will be fine, we assure you.

M: What exactly is happening?

AR: There is so much work that is going on right now—galactic universes, planets, parallel universes, and the angelic realms have all gathered under one cause—the one that has affected humankind and the Universe—love. Never before has there been such a grand union of physical and nonphysical under one idea. You are feeling this, Mary. This is huge. Your Mother Earth is at the head of everything. She is more powerful than you can ever realize. Trust her. Look for ways to connect with her, and she will infuse you with an energy that will surpass anything you have ever experienced.

You have been doing this, as you are taking her into your body. We see that you are changing and enjoying the change. Keep doing this. It will make these meetings happen more frequently.

M: Okay. I will keep doing it. I can feel the energy from the plants and vegetables that I am eating.

AR: Yes, this is the Divine energy of Mother Earth. She is magnificent. Her energy will guide you in your daily actions.

M: Okay. I will. Thank you. Why am I not manifesting the things that I want, especially money?

AR: You have hit a roadblock of sorts. Not to worry. You are recalibrating. You are feeling not like yourself, yes?

M: Yes. Exactly. I feel like I am outside of myself, just simply floating through my life. It is unfamiliar to me, so I am confused and nervous about it. How can I line up with the recalibration?

AR: You cannot do anything about it but receive it. It is lining you up and lining up with you. This is powerful Source energy commanding the future. It has been chosen already by you, so you see, you need not do anything about it. Do not worry. You will soon begin to feel a sense of familiarity with yourself again, but it will be a new familiarity. Or maybe we should say an old and new familiarity. Many things have been happening around you that have threatened to throw off the desires of humankind. We and many others around you are harnessing Source (light) and aiming it toward you and others. You are feeling its power. This is okay. You need not worry. Keep doing the yoga and meditating. It will help you connect with your body and spirit at the same time. This is important.

M: Why have I been avoiding this journey into the Akashic Records? It used to feel easy for me to access them. I have been avoiding opening them and don't know why.

AR: Your Records show you reaching many forks in your lifetime ... you have certainly passed through several already. Those were your lessons in gaining confidence in your ability to intuitively know where you are to go. You are now directly in front of another of these forks and are feeling the confusion around it more because of the outside forces that are trying to usurp the Universal love plan. Have you noticed how many people you know who are drifting about, feeling anxious or confused? This is a critical time on Earth. Powerful energy is swirling around humankind. Stay close to your Akashic Records, Mary.

M: What next steps do I need to take to move my life forward?

AR: Your creativity is being stepped up right now. You will begin to have more heightened ideas for future projects. Stay with them. Take action on each of them. This is how you can move successfully through this fork. And follow your intuition, which is very strong.

We also want to affirm for you what your recent reading said about you taking on energies from others. Be aware of this. You have absorbed some energies from your partner, Christine. Those energies are part of her path. Be careful to not take hers on. You have absorbed this on an unconscious level, and it has left you feeling not like yourself, right? It has also stopped you from becoming successful. You were like a chameleon in one past life. You could disguise yourself by making yourself look and seem like others around you. This is why you have been struggling through much of this life with not knowing who you really are. In that past life, you were a master of disguise. No one who was searching for you could ever find you. So, you accomplished lots in that lifetime—moving from place to place, creating change, and leaving. This is also why, in this lifetime, you seem to not be present . . . your words have been that you felt like you did not exist when you were little.

Now you can remove your disguises and be you.

M: I am still feeling like I do not belong in New York City right now. I am desiring to live in Los Angeles, near my special spiritual friends and resources. How can I reconcile this if I am supposed to be living here in New York?

AR: You have to find yourself first, Mary. Stay on this journey you and Christine have begun—juicing, eating vegetarian, and practicing yoga and meditation—and begin to write.

Line up with where you really want to live. Line up inside yourself. You must work on taking Christine out of the picture when you are doing this. You have been basing your conclusions on thoughts that include her. This is not how you will be able to discover, not only who you are, but where you are to be next.

We are not saying you should not respect and love Christine—you are two people who are deeply in love. But you must separate from each other when you are doing your deep soul work. She has a path that she has chosen and so have you. Your Records show you two together, but you both have merged your fears without knowing it. Can you feel this?

M: Yes. I know this now.

AR: It will help Christine to visit her Akashic Records often and to find time away from her electronic world and to focus toward Earth—walking, driving to green areas, to the ocean, spending time with the dogs outside in new areas, not old ones—and journaling her responses to these outings. Share this with her. This, too, will help you both.

And Mary, you must spend your time doing joyful, happy things again—research your next motorcycle, go bicycling away from the city, take your bike in the car out to the ocean, and ride with fantastic music blasting into your body. Laugh again. You have become serious, and this is not the energy of your Records, which is why you have been feeling like you are drifting away from the Akashic Records. Your Records will always be there. They have no beginning and no end. They exist forever.

M: Should I be leaving the entertainment industry to pursue something else? If so, how can I discover what that is?

AR: You have chosen the entertainment industry for a reason. It was not a mistake. There are never mistakes. You now need to embrace your creativity in a new way. Let it lead you, Mary. It will guide you gracefully into your next phase. You will understand it as it begins to unfold. Trust us that it will not be difficult. We see you trying too hard to understand everything right now. Trust in your Divine and know that you have the answers to everything deep inside. The reason you have been unhappy is because you are not trusting that it is in you. Just have an awareness of this. Do not try to let your mind figure it out, as your mind is not capable of understanding this. Simply put your mind aside and feel your heart, soul, and inner being . . . that is it. When you are moved by something beautiful . . . that is it. When you are emotional over something that represents love . . . that is it. When you are laughing uncontrollably. . . that is it. At those times, take a second and be aware that this is your inner Divine. You will gradually become so familiar with it that you will no longer require trust, and everything you desire will come to you effortlessly—this is the true path to freedom.

M: Will a book evolve from these Akashic readings?

AR: There is a strong possibility, yes. When you have a sense about a specific topic that will be of interest to readers, bring these questions into your Akashic Records sessions, and we will journey through them with you as we are now doing.

M: I have this feeling to ask my Akashic Records about certain topics, but how does asking for the world relate to my personal Records?

AR: Your Records show you as a teacher, Mary. You will hear enlightened information not only during your personal readings but from the readings of others—information and knowledge that will benefit many. You will recognize it as it is happening.

The Akashic Records are an ethereal space through which all of humanity exists, all at once, all the time . . . your time, that is, since there really is no time.

M: I would like to receive a profound message that can benefit many by my sharing it. Can you give that to me now?

AR: Yes, and remember, Mary, that we are you. You are accessing your Divine soul for this profound message. Be still for a moment, and we will send to you, from you, a profound thought.

> *The powerful energy of love is parting the veil between human and nonphysical in a joyful dance— a dance that joins the common knowing that both sides experience of each other. Nonphysical is*

experiencing physical, and physical is knowing that nonphysical is present. Now that they have been joining together, the ego does not need to be in power. It is simply love. Just love. This is creating a fantastic new energy with a power that both sides can ride on. This joyous interaction is creating the new future of humankind.

M: Thank you. I appreciate this so much, and it has been so good to be back in the Records. I will revisit often, as this is something I have chosen as a path.

AR: You did choose this, Mary. Once you begin to follow the paths you chose for your time on Earth, you will experience immense joy. When humans buck their own currents, they experience pain and confusion, and often illness. This involves more than following your desires. It is about looking inward and listening to your path reveal itself to you. One way to be sure you are going inward, and not allowing your ego to trick you into thinking you are, is to meditate to the point where your mind is at peace—calm, relaxed—in a space where you have no thoughts. We see that this is a challenge for many. Once in this state, you will get in touch with your inner Divine, and from there you will see all paths that you have already chosen and can choose which one you will follow in the present. This is your personal, private Divine storehouse of you. It is blessed and sacred.

I did not realize how much I was holding—how much of what I thought was confusion was actually a quiet rearranging beneath the surface. In this exchange, I did not receive a plan; I received a reactivation of sorts. The Akashic Records mirror who we are. I experienced a version of myself that has always been within me and that I am now remembering.

WHY THE AKASHIC RECORDS
ALWAYS SPEAK TO NOW

I'VE OFTEN WONDERED why it is that each time I reread my Akashic Records exchanges, the messages feel new, alive, and resonate so deeply with my current moment. When I asked the Records about this, the answer was beautifully clear—the Akashic Realm reflects our soul's chosen design, moment by moment. Every shift we experience, every choice we make, is imprinted in our Akashic Records. So when we return to them, we are not revisiting the past; we are meeting our Divine self exactly where we are, in the now.

M: Why is it that when I reread my Akashic Records sessions, it is as if the messages are new?

AR: This is the power of Divine. Its energy reflects the All-That-Isness of life itself at every given moment. Human life shifts and changes, and as it does, it becomes recorded in the Akashic Records as an ethereal imprint. When you open your Records, you receive all imprints at once. Remember that your Akashic Records are a direct mirror of you. The Records do not exist in your time. They are quantum—a Divine living organism of you. As you move through the events of your life, making choices along the way, your Divinity moves along with you, recording everything. When you stop to enter this Realm, you are stepping into your own living energy, and as you set yourself up to receive from your own Akashic

Records, that permission flows the Divine energy into you. The words that come through, whether through recorded dialogue or writing, become the carrier of your Divine power. Remember that energy never dies. It moves about, along with the shifts and changes that a person experiences. What makes the Akashic Records so powerful as a tool is that they are an endless reflection of each soul's chosen journey. That is what the Divine Realm is designed for. A human cannot throw off their soul's original chosen path. That part is fixed. They can, however, veer away from it, through the various choices that they make throughout their lives. However, the design of humans is so magnificent that they will receive signs when this happens. One way to click back into a chosen path is to allow the energy of the Akashic Records to flow through to you. Each time you reread or listen back to your readings, because it is a Divine reflection of you at every given moment, it will reflect to you your design, your chosen path, in the way that your present moment can receive the "reminder." The reason it feels so good to be in your Akashic Records is that you are being immersed in your own light—uninterrupted or uninfluenced by anything outside of you. The Masters, Teachers, and Loved Ones, as the keepers of your Records, see to this. It is a magnificent design from God/Source!

My own life is a testament to what the Divine Realm conveys here. I came to realize that my destiny was far more layered than I originally believed and that it included everything I'd ever done. Things began to come together in a way that made sense once I started looking at my life through the lens of my Akashic Records.

What I've learned is that when things do not seem to be working, it is often a sign that we have drifted from our chosen path.

I have experienced this myself, and when I've worked with these concerns in my Akashic Records, I discovered something deeper within me that was ready to emerge. I've learned that these deeper discoveries are always connected to everything we have chosen across lifetimes. There are no mistakes. The Records remind us of this each time we return to them.

MINUSCULE INSTANT
OF KNOWING

I WAS EXPERIENCING physical sensations that were unfamiliar and puzzling. My perception was that something was wrong with me. I opened my Records for clarity, and again, the profound messages not only soothed me around this particular issue, but they also affirmed my chosen role in this lifetime. This is what occurs in many of my clients' Akashic Records sessions—they come to their Records with a particular question or a specific issue, and before the end of the session, any further questions they had hoped would be answered have already been answered! Here was my reading.

M: I have some questions regarding my physical issues that I would like to address.

AR: We know it has been a struggle for you to return to this place of dialogue. No need to worry, Mary. There is so much happening around your planet these days, much too much for your third-dimensional world to be able to grasp. Please know that the physical sensations you are experiencing are all a result of this shift in energy that is taking place.

M: I will try to relax into it more. But what can I do to alleviate these strange and unknown physical feelings I am having?

AR: Make a daily practice of opening these, your Akashic Records, and engage each day in a dialogue with us, your

Masters, Teachers, and Loved Ones. You are a natural at this, Mary, because you entered your third-dimensional realm already having the comfort level around this kind of dialogue. You have always sensed things. Others labeled it as sensitive, but once you begin to utilize this as your gift, your life will soar. Practice being comfortable in this space.

M: Okay. Some more specific questions now. First, what is this dull hearing in my left ear about? Is it an allergy, something for me to be concerned about?

AR: Major shift for you, Mary. Your reality is going to continue to change, and it may feel uncomfortable to you for some time. Please be patient, and keep your focus on the future, your future. Your body is trying to revolt against the changes. This is why it is important for you to practice dialoguing in this sacred space. We will give to you what you need as you travel through this planetary change. Trust us. We love you beyond your worldly words. We can work on you during these conversations.

M: I give you my permission to work on me. Is there some way that I will recognize that something has taken place?

AR: Yes, you will feel like laughing. We threw you with that one, yes?

M: Yes, you did. Laughter?

AR: We know that laughter is for you the best way to allow information from other dimensions. It cracks a tunnel wide open around you. Remember that every time you feel the urge to laugh, we are working on your body and soul, fine-tuning it, so you will be better able to travel within the dimensions.

Mary, you agreed to come to this third-dimensional planet to guide others past the third dimension into their other realms and dimensions. People trust you because you are truthful and lead with your heart. You are not afraid to share from your heart. This sets up a flowing relationship with others for them to feel safe in uncomfortable situations.

M: Sometimes it feels as if I am the one writing these dialogues—that it is coming from my head. Help me clarify the difference.

AR: Firstly, you indeed are writing these sessions, but the difference is that you are receiving a transmission of thoughts and ideas from the outside. Does it feel like that right now?

M: Yes, actually, it does. It is a strange feeling to somehow be present yet be receiving.

AR: Yes, and this is why we want you to frequent this space, so you will cease to question its validity. The questioning is your ego stepping in, to figure things out and take control. Thank it and continue to listen to what appears to be on the outside.

M: I am still a bit hooked on these physical problems I am experiencing. What specifically can I do?

AR: Tap into that stream and know that you will receive exactly what you need to do. The specifics will come to you. You will know that it is from the streams of Source in the exact instant that you think of them.

Remember, there is a minuscule instant of knowing that appears before you when you are trying to make a decision. This is the Source field. It is not intuition. It is not intention. It is not your mind. It is not even your body. It is the field. That field is feeding you constantly. Most humans do not know how to act on those moments, because at that exact minuscule instant, their minds jump in to interpret what has just occurred, and they are next led away from the exact action they were given. We know you know this and are ready to home in on this skill. You have been sensing the future. Yes?

M: I think I have been having small windows of this, yes?

AR: Yes. In those moments—those minuscule moments which seem like flashes—try acting immediately on them. Immediately. Do not tell anyone. Test this, so you will understand the reality of what we are saying here. It is like being on that perfect spot on a huge wave—as soon as you think about it, you fall. When you try this exercise, remember to write it down and write the outcome of the action. We know you know this minuscule window we speak of.

We promise to be by your side now that you understand that we are here and what the Akashic field is really about. We will assure you that your life will feel better and better. Follow the signs you get in those minuscule flashes of insight, and take actions based on those insights. You will smile at the accuracy that exists. This accuracy is all there is in the Divine Realm beyond the third dimension. There are no mistakes—only love and bliss. Mistakes are not real, just interpretations of the ego to keep it in existence. All is always well, as are you, Mary. These are major shifts you are experiencing.

M: How can I find my passion again for things? I feel as if I have lost my purpose here, and it feels weird—like my life is beginning to be over.

AR: Yes, your third-dimensional life is beginning to end, but not the way you think. You are not dying, Mary. There is so much that is written in your Records for this period in your soul's journey. But you are shedding third-dimensional things: third-dimensional thoughts and solutions. The passions you felt before were third-dimensional passions, not true passion. True passion is you sitting here right in this moment, having this dialogue with us (with YOU). We invite you to cross over into this place on a regular basis. Do not be afraid. You are not going to disappear, although you have already been disappearing to many, but that is because they are staying behind in the energy of the third dimension. Just know, Mary, that you are exactly where you planned to be, right on time, right now. Stay on the journey. Your body will line up with you. Love it like crazy. Laugh at it, play with it, share it with your loved ones. It is not something separate from you, it is merely the third-dimensional aspect of you. That is all. And because it is part of the whole you, it is of love, came from love, continues to live in love, and will continue, on and on, even after it dissolves. It will reinvent itself in your next lifetime—so beautiful, so wonderful, so magnificent.

M: Wow…thank you. So beautiful. I can feel the stream of love right now.

This exchange reminded me that what I had been feeling physically was not and is not random. It's connected to something much bigger that is unfolding on both a personal and planetary level. I am not broken—I am adjusting—and I don't have to control the process. I just need to stay connected and open. I was also reminded that I've always had a sensitivity to energy. It is not something to fix or hide—it is something to honor. The more I spend time in the Akashic Records, the more I experience a trust that feels like it is outside of me and within me simultaneously. And with that comes a deeper understanding of how profoundly supported I am by the Divine itself.

INTUITION IS THE ANSWER TO EVERYTHING

A T T H E T I M E of this Akashic Records exchange, I was feeling restless—unsettled in my environment, unclear about what was next, and disconnected from my creative center. New York City—once vibrant and energizing—had begun to feel heavy and misaligned. I opened my Records hoping for clarity and received more than answers; I received an invitation to release outdated ways of deciding, moving, and creating. This exchange became a turning point for me. I began to see how much of my life had been shaped by logic and structure, and that it was time to surrender to the exact moment of intuition.

M: I've been feeling lost here in my New York City—my apartment, my neighborhood. What is this about? My last reading suggested that I needed to be here.

AR: And that was indeed true. Look at and take inventory of the things that have happened that are important to you in this lifetime. You reconnected with important individuals. You reinvented your career—or re-motored it. You made new friends. Now it is time for change, and you must make the choice. Do not be afraid of it. There are never wrong choices, simply choices.

M: Am I supposed to move away from here? Away from New York City?

AR: Absolutely yes, Mary. The environment around you is shifting and changing as part of the shifts and changes that are occurring on Earth as a whole. As things in parts of the world become elevated, an equal number of things in other parts of the world become lower—closer to 3D. The elevated places are already away from 3D, moving rapidly through other dimensions. It is your time to be in those areas.

M: Where are these areas?

AR: You must find them. You are sensing strongly that you are being called somewhere. You are correct. Follow your deepest sense of where you are to be. We can tell you that your struggle is related to your old beliefs around logical thinking—one thought leads to another, which leads to yet another—and you trust that, through this process, you will arrive at the right decision or place. This is why you do not mind "not knowing" what lies ahead. You are used to trusting in your thought process. You feel something or experience something very profound . . . then it gets immediately transferred to your mind . . . your mind then deciphers it and figures out what is next. What we would like you to do is to jump right from what you first feel directly into action.

M: Wow. This is huge for me.

AR: Yes, you have tricked yourself into thinking you are in control of following your intuition—you are not. You have a keen sense of your intuition, but you have not harnessed its power. Intuition is the answer to everything in humankind. It has been glossed over as an initial feeling about something. It is so much more than that. Intuition is love energy on the run—just ride it. Jump on it and ride. Your mind has tricked you into thinking that you should be doing certain things. And you have drifted away from your soul journey as a result. This is why you are so confused—why you say that you are in limbo. There is no such thing as limbo. It has never existed. There is perceived space. Even space is not real. There is always love vibrating through everything—in powerful colors and energies.

M: I just had an atmosphere change in my left ear.

AR: Welcome back, Mary.

M: Yes. I am familiar with this wonderful energy. It is so light and easy and loving and simple, yet profound.

AR: Yes. You are basking in the field. Remember, Mary, you are a writer. You are a teller of stories, passing on love tucked under words and ideas. As the words and ideas are released, the love begins to ooze up and out into the Universe. This is the power of storytelling. You are here to do this. We once shared with you that when you begin to write, it will be so easy and that we will be there with you.

M: Why is it so hard for me to write? I don't know what's in the way.

AR: Fear, Mary. You are afraid to let go of what you have been in your career in your past. You are afraid to release the director part of your career. But this is emanating from an old belief system. You were identified as a director, which is all well and good. But you are not ready to move on to your next phase of creation. It will be okay. You do not have to worry about money. It will always be there for you.

Begin each morning, starting tomorrow, by writing about something that feels fun and carefree. Your newest idea, we see, gives you pleasure. Start with that. Use the new software program that you recently purchased to guide you some. You can also open your Records and begin to write the story. We will not be in dialogue in this way with you, but instead, you will feel our presence, and that will be enough. Try this and see what magnificence you will experience. We assure you that this writing time each day will feel wonderful and invigorating to you.

M: Okay. I will try this tomorrow morning. What about the jobs I have been trying to get recently? Should I keep pursuing those shows?

AR: This is, of course, your decision. Whatever you focus on, you will bring to you. You are an immensely powerful manifester. We can see that you find it pleasurable to see yourself directing new shows with new groups of people. If this is what you want for now, then you must line up with it and go for it.

Your intuition may be telling you something else. You must listen to your intuition and jump into action based on it. Do not wait for your mind to picture what you think you want.

M: I am confused now. I thought you said I was to let that career go.

AR: Your Records show you moving through several careers. Remember that you have been extremely successful in your directing career. There is a completion about it that you may be avoiding. It is not an end. And, unless you move through it and on to your next quests, you will remain in the same place, which is what we are sensing from you. Fly, Mary. Take the leap that your soul is driving you toward. It is good that you are going to Los Angeles. You will soak up the energy from there, which will be good for you right now.

We assure you that if you take a small amount of time each day to either meditate or open your Records briefly, your next decisions will become clear and easy. We cannot tell you what to do, but we can reflect to you what your Records are telling us about you and your journey.

Your journey in your present lifetime is guiding you to be a loving reflection of the most beautiful parts of others. This is what you came here to do and what you chose to be in this lifetime. It is so easy for you and so natural that you do not realize that you could have a career doing just this and be extremely wealthy as well. Begin to flourish in the knowledge of this. When you flourish inside, you will bring wealth to you. It will feel easy because it is easy. When things become difficult, it is because you are not listening to or following your soul's journey. Let that be your "forever clue." It will tell you, each time it happens, to look elsewhere.

M: Is Los Angeles a good area for me?

AR: Los Angeles nurtures you. You have many resources there that can nourish your soul. You must decide. Try to take some quiet time while you are there to "listen" to what your intuition tells you. You have been distracted by the thought that Christine is not wanting what you are wanting. Let this go. Listen to YOU. If you do not, you will become sick.

M: Wow.

AR: You are not surprised. We know you know this. It is quite easy to get distracted in New York City. The energy in the city is moving at lightning speed, so fast that there is little time to stop and listen. This is why the people there are not hearing their hearts. It is too fast-moving. Thoughts are flying about, colliding with each other. When alignment occurs in this fast field, there are immediate successes. This is why there is such a divide between the wealthy and the poor. Some collide with the energy and get lost, and some align with it and ride as fast as it can go. So, New York is a wonderful place for some and not so wonderful for others. This is why it was such a successful place for you many years ago. You were attracted by the fast energy, and you joined it. It benefited you. You are now attracted to a more subtle and powerful stream—the stream that exists outside of the fast stream. When you can focus your energy outside of it, or above it, you miss the opportunities that exist inside, the energy that is flying by. This looks like missed opportunities to you, but it is just that you are now more aligned with what is happening above and outside of it. Above and outside is where discoveries come from. It is where ideas are born. It is where the creative force is born, like a seed about to sprout.

M: This is interesting to me. I *have* been feeling as if I've been missing opportunities. And it makes sense now. I am banging around in the wrong field of energy.

AR: Yes. And this is why the job at certain television networks did not work out for you. You looked upon these events as a failure. However, it was simply you, beginning to move into a different energy realm. Do not be afraid to take the leap into the new realm, Mary. We will support you. And stay connected to your Records as you do, since this is a foreign "field" to you. It is not third-dimensionally based. It is above the third dimension. Once you begin to align yourself there, all decisions will come easily to you. Your body will react positively as well. You will sleep more and enjoy life more.

M: Okay. I will begin to take notice of these things. I am feeling blank right now. What happened?

AR: You drifted away, which is a good thing. Do you remember what you were thinking just then?

M: No. I got really relaxed and felt calmly blank.

AR: Great. This is the area we are speaking of. You are quietly listening to the energy field outside and above the faster stream that we were referring to. Do not be afraid to sit in this field without doing a thing. Then take notice of how you feel after.

M: I will.

AR: What else do you want to know now?

M: Still blank.

AR: Take a few moments right now. Stop typing and relax into that space . . . then come back and write exactly the first thing that you feel or sense.

M: Okay . . . I feel safe, warm, and relaxed. And both my ears are humming . . . like mild "atmosphere."

AR: Yes, this is the area we are referring to. Try to spend time there and go deeper into it when you can. You will come out with a better sense of what you are to do next in your life.

Try this tomorrow morning and make sure to write—fiction, not a diary. Write what comes to your mind first, no matter how absurd or strange. This will be a wonderful exercise for you.

And try not to look at your actions recently as failures. You needed to be immersed in this fast field in order to find what is above and outside of it. You are now ready to jump in. We can sense this for you.

M: Okay. Thank you for this time, and it is so good to be back receiving this energy and information again.

AR: We are always here, Mary, and always in Divine love with you.

I had been used to relying on my mind to make sense of things. But what I'm learning is that intuition doesn't need to be translated; it just needs to be followed—quickly, quietly, without overthinking.

This dialogue helped me see that I wasn't lost; I was simply between frequencies. The restlessness, the blankness, even the sense of failure were not signs that I was off track—they were just part of the shedding of an old way of operating. And I discovered that the new way is within me—*The Akashic Way*. This is what is so beautiful about spending time in the Akashic Records. The loving essence of the light of Divine washes over us to reveal the beauty that we are.

MY LOVED ONES ON THE OTHER SIDE

THE MASTERS, TEACHERS, and Loved Ones are the light energies that oversee and protect the integrity of our Akashic Records. They are with us—always. As a reminder, the Loved Ones are those energies we have experienced love with during our present lifetime who are now on the other side—family, teachers, friends, partners—anyone.

I decided to share this visitation from two of my loved ones on the other side—my mother and brother—during one of my Akashic readings as an example of how our loved ones can show up and participate in our Akashic exchanges. We experience our loved ones differently within the Akashic Records. They are holding the Divine light of our Records, communicating with us from that light that is our soul. Their role is as a collective of love energy—maintaining the integrity of our soul's chosen path. They will communicate in a way that feels comfortable and recognizable to us.

I was grieving very much from the loss of my mother and dear brother Ronald, and the weight of this grief was so heavy. After this exchange, I experienced a lightness of being that amazed me. Since then, my grief has transformed itself into a more powerful relationship with both my mother and brother on the other side. I also have a sense of ease about what happens after we transition. The following exchange, although deeply personal, shines a light on the other side—and the pure love that exists there. Here is that reading:

M: Being in the Akashic field is much more than comfortable. I can feel my loved ones—my mother, my brother, and my beloved pets—when I am in this space. I feel them all at once and individually, at the same time. It's very strange, but so comforting too.

AR: Yes, they are all here. You can feel their essence—the best of who they were in your life and theirs—as well as their true essence where they are right now, in this field of love. They are speaking with you right now, and we are honored to participate in it with you. Speak with them now. We will step aside . . .

M: Mommy, are you here?

Mom: Yes, Mary, I am here. I have been here all along. I know you have been in much pain over me. I am here to tell you that you need not be. I am so happy here. It is so magnificent, Mary. You remember when I would share my dreams with you about seeing green fields forever? It is so much better than that. It is everything all at once . . . no time . . . no limits . . . just freedom, forever freedom. I have seen your struggles, and I want you to know that I have been over your shoulder every step of the way and will always be. Our journey was short, but it was what we both agreed to before coming to Earth. We were living our choices together, and what a wonderful time I had with you. I thoroughly enjoyed every single moment we had together, from the first moment you were born from me. You were my angel, Mary. I do not mean to make you upset, but you need to hear from me. You need to be strong, Mary. It is time for you to be strong, as you are going to have many challenges that will require your strength—physical, mental, and spiritual. You will exceed your own expectations. This I always knew about you when you were first born. I knew you had come from God, and I loved you so much—more than you will ever know. You and I will be reunited once again, and it will be so beautiful. I will be here to take you into my arms once again as you cross over. But do not think about this now, Mary, for you have much more to do down there on Earth. I can feel you feel me. The connection we are having is exactly the connection we both had when I carried you in my womb. Feel it? This is why you did not want to come out. We were both so in love with our connection. I, too, did not want you to come out. I wanted to hold on to what we both had, so you see, your being breech was not just you, it was me too. You were my Divine salvation on Earth, Mary, and now I am telling you that I am your Divine salvation for the rest of your years on Earth. Come to me anytime, whether in this Akashic Realm or anywhere else. I am always with you. I love you so, my Mary. Now, be calm and know all is well. Now that you are speaking with us in this way, I wish for you to experience Ronald, whom I know you are thinking about. Yes, Mary, he is here too. We are together in love and light.

M: Ronald, can you speak with me?

Ronald: Yes. I am here, Mary. Please do not be so upset. There is nothing to be upset about. I am so happy where I am now. This place is amazing. Everyone we know exists here, everyone. There is no pain, there are no worries . . . just joy. You and I experienced lots of joy together. Multiply that by millions. I have been hanging around you lots. I know you have been feeling me. Yes, it has been me. I want to make sure that you know I am always with you and that I love you so much.

M: I love you, too, Ronald. I wish so much that we had more time together.

Ronald: Yes, I know. But we were both carrying out our missions on Earth. Mine was one of lessons learned and things cleared away from past lives. I am now clear, Mary. So clear. It is amazing. It feels like purity, pure purity, and yes, all the animals are here too. It is like a continuous party of love and beauty, never-ending, no time, no restrictions, no problems, just love. I feel so much better being here. It was a tough transition for me. I was so resistant, and I am sorry you had to experience this with me, as this is what I left you with. But please know that once I let go, it was pure heaven. I did see Mommy as I was leaving. She was right there to guide me from my body. She was beautiful, Mary. You will one day have a vision of Mommy as I saw her when I was leaving. She smiled and reached for me. I thought for a moment that she was going to leave without me. This was when Christine heard me call out to Mommy. I did, but she was still there. I saw her beautiful blue eyes, and she smiled right at me. It was then that I knew what was happening. I knew I was to go, so I released and went. It felt like flying, up and up. She held me in a way I had never experienced before, and it was so wonderful to be held by her. It was hard for me to go, as I saw the pain you and Christine were experiencing, but I knew it was my destiny that I had to follow. It is just how it is, this Divine plan. Mary, please know that I will never leave you. You were the one left behind, and we know this is hard for you. So, we promise you right now that we are here for you . . . always. Just call us, and we will show you we are here. Okay? You are doing a fantastic job right now, allowing this communication to come through. I know how hard it is. I can feel your pain and sadness. Do not worry and do not be sad. I wish we could see each other as I know you want to see me and Mommy, but this is the way of the Divine. We must find new ways to "see" each other, and we will. It will be okay. This will all become clearer for you as your time goes on. Be patient, and always call on me, as I am here, always, for you. I love you more than you know. This Divine love that I am floating in is much more powerful than you can imagine. I am here to tell you that there is a God. It is amazing, Mary. I always knew there was a God, but I never knew how hugely wonderful it was—until I transitioned. Do not be afraid of this. It is all good. Always come to this Akashic Realm, and we will continue to experience our new relationship, our new Divine relationship. I know you do not want to leave me right now, but we must. You have obligations for the rest of the day. I love you. I love you. I love you. Remember how many times I used to say this to you? I am saying it again and again, a thousandfold. You are part of me, and I am part of you, always and forever.

Your loving brother, Ronald.

M: Thank you both for showing up for me. I am so emotional right now. I can't even see this page clearly. I'm so grateful and honored to be in this presence right now.

AR: Yes, Mary, we, your Master and Teachers, have returned. We are so happy that you were able to have the courage to communicate and receive from your loved ones. There are more here, but for another time. We knew this would be the right time for you to experience this family love. As your Master, I am here to mirror to you how so loved you are. Take this knowledge with you. Make your decisions and conclusions from this realm. All is well. There are no problems, ever. We are here to gently guide you back to center whenever you reach out and need it. We are the keepers of your Divine rights, your Divine pasts, and your Divine futures.

We are in love with you.

There is so much beauty in this last exchange. At first, the reading was very painful for me because my grief was still so raw. However, as I reached the end, the pain had transformed into ease and grace. I felt so good, so real, and so loved. It was Divine love. And, as another reminder about the timelessness of these Divine exchanges, each time I reread this exchange, I can feel my mother and brother right next to me.

THE EGO SOUP

THERE WAS A PERIOD when I kept receiving the message that I would be awakened around 2 or 3 a.m. to receive important downloads. At first, I resisted, concerned I wouldn't be able to function without a full night's sleep. But something inside nudged me to trust. This exchange with my Akashic Records reshaped how I view rest, creativity, and the energetic landscape we live in.

In these quiet hours, when the world around me slept, I came to understand that this was more than just a writing practice—it was a dismantling. I learned how the ego cloaks itself in clever disguises, blending with collective fear until it becomes what the Records refer to as a massive ego soup. This dense energy feeds off distraction, division, and disconnection. But the Earth and Divine Mother offer a nourishment that awakens the soul—not the ego.

What I learned through this reading changed how I live, how I write, and how I understand my energy in relationship to the world around me.

AR: Your schedule around this writing will be no schedule at all, and do not worry about not getting enough sleep. You will be energized always, and when you need to sleep, let your body tell you so. The idea of when people must sleep is another human-invented concept. And it is easier to download ideas when most humans in your area where you live are asleep. They, too, are receiving downloads of information at a crucial time in your world. Portals are open right now.

We want you to also know that these downloads are not always necessarily coming from above you. They are often coming from below you, Mary. Beneath your feet, the energy of light in the form of ideas and solutions is being given to many of you from Earth herself. This is why it is so important to plant your feet on the Earth and let in her love. Earth is holding humanity beyond what you can imagine. She is nourishing you, calling your attention to her through her beauty as well as catastrophic events and weather changes, and offering amazing healing and balance on a regular basis.

M: Is this the same energy as the Divine Mother?

AR: Actually, your Earth is a direct manifestation of the Divine Mother. The Divine Mother encompasses all of humanity, in all its forms—third dimension and beyond. The dimensions, the Akashic Realm, the cosmos—everything sits within the powerful, loving Divine Mother matrix.

There is a web of connectivity. It is part of the absoluteness of all. Imagine this web as millions and millions of crystalline light beams shooting out and pulsating at lightning speed. This continuous pulse is the Divine Mother in her magnificence—love to the Nth degree, if you can imagine. This is the God/Source that drives all humankind, both living and in spirit. As humans live and breathe within this Divine matrix, their etherealness expands immensely. As humans, you cannot comprehend this because you are driven by the ideas (pun here) that your minds are driving you, thriving you. This could not be less true.

M: Do we need to become aware of this Divine matrix?

AR: It is almost better to not, right now in your history. Awareness tends to pitch humans right into the mind-ness of interpretation. This is dangerous because then ego-infused perceptions can follow, and misinterpretations occur. This is why your world feels so topsy-turvy right now. Humans still think that they are running the show. The truth is that humankind becoming the show is true heaven and true Divine. The Divine choreography is now and has always existed. There is no beginning, no middle, or end. It has a perfection to it (words we think you will understand, although there is no perfection). We wish for you all to begin to understand the things you are experiencing that cannot be explained.

M: Like what kinds of things?

AR: Like your recent election, which seems to be turning everyone inside out. This is a giant ego run rampant. Not a singular ego but a collective ego that has been formed from individual upon individual on your Earth, operating from that part of themselves. Over time, when humans allow their ego-centralized ideas, concepts, and actions to run their lives, a giant metaphorical soup is created. This soup gets warmer, then hotter, then boils over, and when it does, it affects the whole of humanity. This is a crucial time in your history.

Everyone is basically getting hit with their own ego soup. There is not one human being on your planet who has not in some way participated in this ego overflow. Those of you who claim having no part in this are, in fact, feeding into it even more. The claim that one could not have poissibly (yes, this word . . . poison + possibility) participated in this is exactly the kind of thought that contributed to the ego overflow to begin with. We encourage an understanding of this. To say, "but this cannot be me, because I would never take actions such as this one or that one," sets up a "me and them" idea. "Me and them" or "me versus them" is ego.

Once this is triggered, the only way through it is to allow it. We do not mean to drink this soup as many are engaging in right now. This is a massive ego soup. We cannot express to you how large it really is, for you would become too over-whelmed—and by thinking about its massiveness, you would encourage its growth.

Remember that the ego is not real, so therefore this soup is really an illusion. It has become so big that it has master-fully convinced humankind that it is real and powerful. It is the belief in it that will make it powerful. When one believes in the ego soup, it secretly energizes each individual's per-ceived ego, which then feeds back into the soup and adds to its expansion.

So, the best way right now to emerge out from the other side of this giant ego state is to activate your Divine inner self that knows this is not real.

Notice what is happening with those who are supporting and loving each other, often loving even those whom they are not close to or even know. These actions are actions of the Divine in each person reaching out, spreading out love. When more and more humans come together in this way, the ego soup will lose its perceived nourishment. Those who are en-gaged in its energy will begin to not be nourished by it. And this soup will become stagnant, old, and will rot away.

Please know too that those who are drinking this ego soup are perceiving it as a necessary nourishment. It may actual-ly be nourishing them, but it is nourishing the parts of them that are ego-based and nonexistent. Ego is a tricky concoc-tion, and one that we will be exchanging ideas about for quite some time.

Another message about the ego—it is fear disguising itself as love.

We are unraveling for you this deep concept of the ego itself. Everything in the Universe is love . . . everything! The ego, actually, is love, but it does not know that it is love yet. The ego fears that if it recognizes itself as love and allows itself to experience itself as Divine love, it will poof out of existence. And this is true. So, it fears the thing that it is. To prevent itself from poofing out of existence, it takes on a sort of disguise of love and tricks humans into thinking things are of love when they are not. The ego would not be able to accomplish this if it did not keep this thing called love outside of itself. The ego recognizes that humanity is attracted to and thrives on love. So, it disguises itself as that love. If it understood that it is itself already love, it would no longer exist. Just love would exist.

When an individual, for example, is struggling with (perceived) weight issues, during these low self-image perceptions, the ego tries to hold on for dear life as it encourages more thoughts about low self-worth (non-love). The ego fears that if that individual becomes healthy and fit (self-love), they will not need the ego anymore. This is true!

During these and similar instances, we suggest you talk to your ego. It is not bad. And you may say, "But you said the ego is not real." It is the perception of it that makes it appear real and keeps it relevant, and oftentimes very powerful. So, in the example of the individual struggling with low self-image, the tricky ego will disguise itself as love, and that individual will not realize that he or she is actually in the grips of the ego. That version of love is the ego's own perception of love— its disguise—which is not true love. When that individual responds to the disguise, it will encourage unhealthy choices. If and when that person understands this, then they will be able to powerfully differentiate between this disguised-as-love ego and true Divine love itself. The reality is that once the individual understands this, the ego will lose its grip, and that individual will experience the Divine love that exists inside, which will, in turn, generate healthy, inspired actions, for example, around their body, and the weight will come off, and they will look young, healthy, and thin.

We suggest that you speak to the Divine love inside of your DNA and your cells before going to sleep each night. Surrender all confusing thoughts or uncertainty around any issue in your life to this Divine love. During your sleep time, your body—your DNA—will speak to the rest of you and fix things that are out of balance. You know this. Just live it now. You will then become inspired to take actions that will contribute to health, wholeness, and self-expansion.

M: Are there other ways to dissipate the energy of this ego soup?

AR: Yes, many. Humans have more Divine tools than they realize. We will begin to help you remember them now.

Love, of course—in all pure forms—is the biggest tool of them all. However, it is sometimes difficult for those who are merely sipping on the ego soup, and not completely immersed in it, to find the love that they have inside themselves. This is okay because there are so many other tools available.

Ancient wisdom holds the keys to understanding everything of which we speak. There are more examples and concepts that can eradicate this ego soup in a flash. Your ancient times experienced this same ego-collective state, sometimes in greater ways, if you can imagine. There are mystics and ascended beings on your planet right now who are bringing forward these ancient wisdom solutions, in the form of ideas.

Seek them and let in what they are offering. Research your indigenous cultures and learn how they live and how they communicate with each other and with the planet.

Connect to Divine Mother Earth as much as possible—this means her oceans, too. Walk the Earth, touch her as much as possible, swim in her oceans, stand at your ocean's edges, and breathe her energy into and through you. Talk with the creatures that are living in them. They hear you, and they operate only from Divine love. This will create a reactivation, an expansion in you that you may not feel right away, but we promise, it will be done.

Be in joy, joy, joy. Be kind to yourselves. Joy is everywhere! You do not have to manufacture it! Just one small perception of joy expands out into the Universe and right back to you.

Create a love affirmation for yourself—a beautiful combination of gratitude and desire in one statement. And look at this every day, many times, if possible. This affirmation should emanate at the precise moment that you are experiencing how special you are. Affirmations can be tricky, too. Most humans create affirmations out of need (ego), fear (ego), and perceived lack (ego), and they then wonder why they have not manifested. The magic in affirmations lies in the state you are in when you create them. When you are experiencing your love essence, at that precise moment, write your affirmation. This affirmation tool creates a wave of healthy self-love that emanates into the Universe, and more expansion, which gives less and less power to the ego soup.

This exchange reminded me how easily we can mistake ego-driven thought for truth. The concept of the ego soup helped me understand how the more we buy into collective fear and separation, the stronger they become. The ego is not just personal;

it grows into a collective ego that feeds off judgment, comparison, and disconnection. We can see evidence of this throughout our world today.

The Divine truth that reignited in me was this: The ego does not need to be fought. It simply needs to be recognized for what it is, and the more we acknowledge our inner Divine, the less hold ego has. Connecting with the Earth, practicing joy, creating from love, not fear—these are the ways we dissolve the illusion.

TRICKS OF THE EGO

THERE ARE MOMENTS when music becomes more than sound. It opens a portal. During a particular listening experience, I felt something shift. It was subtle at first, then unmistakable. I was being held by the energy of Mother Earth. It was a kind of love I had not experienced before—pure, effortless, cosmic. Through this journey into my Records, I began to understand more about what I was feeling and how it relates to ego, love, and my role in the world. This exchange was a layered, personal dialogue that bridged Earth's wisdom with the Divine light of the Akashic Realm.

M: I really felt Mother Earth's energy *loving me*. Or maybe she was reflecting my love back to me? It is such a special kind of love, this feeling.

AR: Yes, you were experiencing the love from the cosmic field that exists always beyond your material world. Your material world can carry this love, or we should say, bounce it off itself into you humans. This is why humans have a strong attraction to things. Certain things have actually been placed on your Earth to motivate you all into a love energy. This is why we stress that material things are not bad. We refer to the material things that bring you joy, of course, for when you are joyful, then you are pumping in and out that cosmic love, which expands the Universe.

M: Wow. I love that. It is what I have always felt. So, it has to do with what happens during our relationship with these material things?

AR: Exactly. If you allow them to push you into your ego place, then they are not serving you anymore. It is good to have an awareness of this. This is also true for relationships. If your relationships—personal or business—are helping you to focus on negative things, whether it is about them or you, then they are not serving you. You must seek ways to be guided back to your inner soul, that place that literally and only holds love for everything. We see that this word love seems to have many interpretations and sometimes becomes trapped in a cage that the ego has created. This is what you all call evil. There is no evil—which we know you know. There is the place where actions emerge from the ego. The ego is false all the time. It does not even exist. It is a creation of man, and it is not real.

During this same reading, I addressed my struggles around a big project I was working on that I felt perplexed about.

AR: This is part of the weaving in and out that is happening on your Earth plane right now. Many are experiencing incongruities in behavior, and they are right. Your Earth is, in fact, shifting at lightning speed. It cannot not have a significant effect on you. Mary, you are working with people who are struggling with their egos. Have you not noticed this? Look at your time in this Earth period. We mean this lifetime for you. From your family to your friends to your personal relationships, you are consistently put up against ego-deeds.

M: Powerful word. I almost retyped it, but you really meant that word, yes?

AR: Absolutely, we did. You chose to come into this life to shift people out of their manufactured ego (deeds) and back to love. Have you ever noticed that people in your world are consistently telling you their stories, their troubles? These people have been guided to you to help them dissolve the lies of the ego.

M: Yes, I have noticed this, and sometimes I feel exhausted and even slip into my own ego place, because I feel trapped in that energy.

AR: That is okay. Remember, it does not exist! Keep reminding yourself. Your humanness wants to engage in that, but your soul really does not know this. This may be why you feel so uncomfortable when there is un-love appearing around you. One of your past lives was filled with ego. You were basking in it. In that lifetime you chose, as your soul journeyed, to be immersed in this huge lie, for you knew you would be coming forth in the next lifetime to recognize it for what it truly is—a lie. In that lifetime, for you, when you were living in ego, you hurt many, took advantage of many, and died extremely unhappy. You chose your family (today), one filled with ego energy, to be reminded of it, to ride next to it, so you would know that it was no longer yours. Do you see?

M: Wow, I get it now. I feel you are giving me permission.

AR: No, this was your ego coming in. Do you feel it?

M: Yes. I just got it. There is no permission. I own my inner soul's love energy.

AR: No, ego again. There is nothing to own here. It is free, always. It exists at the center of all life on Earth and beyond. True love requires nothing to do about it. It is the most powerful thing that gyrates everything that was ever and will ever be in existence. So, no, you do not own anything—you tap into it, you experience it, you validate it, you laugh with it, you play with it, you reflect it from you. But you have been doing this much in this lifetime because it was the role you chose to come in with.

M: Thank you for the clarification. What is my role (in this project)?

AR: (The project) is an energy you chose to dance with to test your ego. You see how you ride up and down in this project, from feeling the love to feeling trapped in something that you are not a match to? Only you can figure this out. We cannot solve this for you. But we assure you that your answer lies within you. Your soul has already mapped this out. There is a stream of truth inside of you that, when you simply tap into it, will provide you with a well of peace around this topic. We see that it is testing you, pushing you to back out and run. Be careful, Mary, because the part of you that becomes persuaded into ego thoughts and ideas is not real. We promise you this is true. The energy of creating certain scenarios of what is or is not happening outside of you can be dangerous. Then, it is the ego (again, not real) that propels you into unloving acts on yourself that you may choose. It becomes a vicious cycle. You came here to reflect to others unconditional love. That is it! Sometimes, you seem to look for more, but we can tell you the more that you seek comes from staying in that place of reflecting. We do not mean that you are "teaching." You simply emit love, that is it. And the love is the love inside of you. It has nothing to do with coming from the person or persons outside of you. Just reflect it, but do not then retreat. Do not fear the power of it. We think you might be fearing love's power. The manufactured ego fears its power. Do not buy into it!

M: This is deep.

AR: Not for you. You have chosen this. This is a perfect situation for you, as it is challenging you to emit the love regardless of what anyone connected to it does or how they act on their ego. You seem to want to leave it yet still feel a connection. Yes?

M: Yes, which is why I feel so confused about it.

AR: Have you noticed that the dances you have been in, as your time on this Earth is advancing, have become less simple?

M: Yes. This one is not so cut-and-dried—unlike others from the past, when it was much easier to bring some love, recognize that I was not a match, and move on.

AR: You are coming into your light, Mary. When one is not in their inner light of cosmic love, they will bounce in and out of these life-dances with others. Once you solidly embrace your inner light—by this we mean, you accept it, you appreciate it, you love it, you welcome it always—you know it, you wind up living it. Once this happens, there are no situations that you will be in where you will feel conflict (in you, we mean). This is the experience that Earth has been going through for eons—recognizing that there is no reason for any conflict. Ever. There is only love. Conflict mirrors the ego—again, manufactured. Spread this idea: the ego does not exist. It is the acceptance of the idea that there is an ego that has created it. Get it?

M: I am understanding this in a new way. Something feels different.

AR: Yes. It is because your soul's journey is exactly at the point where it should be.

M: What about my relationship, which has seemed strained and difficult recently? Am I to move away from this?

AR: We cannot tell you that. That must come from inside of you. We can tell you that whether this relationship is still part of your life journey or not will be revealed as you begin to practice habits of health and wellness—we mean daily meditations, accessing your Akashic Records on a more regular basis, being around more music, beginning to write your imaginations onto paper or computer, appreciating the wonderful experiences you are having on a daily basis, tapping into the stream of love every day—and, yes, improving your eating habits, which your partner is perfectly lined up with.

Regarding your relationship, we can tell you, certainly, that if you two tap into your inner stream of love—that place where all is always as it should be—you will both excel in your relationship in a way you never have imagined. It cannot be otherwise. Begin by practicing only loving ways of communicating. And when your ego (not real) manufactures unloving actions or words, do not run from it. Stop. Look it—and each other—in the face, and right there, in that moment, have the courage to toss it aside, recognize it is not real, and choose loving thoughts or words. This is a courageous thing to do, but you will see how it will transform your relationship into the lightness and power you felt when you two first met (this time). Yes, you both knew each other, very deeply, from another lifetime—you are remembering this—and you chose to meet up again, to bring forth new lessons about love and relationships onto this Earth plane. Once you both recognize which thoughts are from the manufactured "ego" (of "ago"), you will not have the need to feed it. Just the awareness will dissolve it. We have been stressing over and over here that it, ego, IS NOT REAL. It is similar to bubbles. When you see them, they are real bubbles (seeing them makes them real), but when you step up and into them, they pop and disappear. You cannot hold on to them. This is the ego. Look at it, step through it with love, and it will pop immediately into nonexistence.

This exchange invited me to understand ego not just as a psychological concept but as an energetic distortion—a temporary illusion that separates us from our natural state of love. What resonated most was the reminder that the ego has no real existence unless we validate it. And when I do validate it, I feel it at once: the contraction, the confusion, the inner conflict. But when I return to the stream of love within me, something softens. I remember who I am. I remember why I am here.

Whether in my creative projects, relationships, or daily thoughts, I now notice the subtle moment when I can either feed the illusion or reflect the love I came here to be. The Akashic Records continue to teach me that my purpose is not to control, fix, or teach, but simply to reflect light. And in that reflection, the healing happens.

SHAME

THIS AKASHIC EXCHANGE began with my concern about a pattern I was noticing throughout my working relationships. What I believed was an issue of external relationships turned out to be rooted in something that I was holding on to—shame. The revelation that it was not even mine to begin with was both liberating and healing.

This chapter offers a deep Akashic perspective on shame: how it is formed, how it can hide in our subconscious or become buried in a past life, and how it can subtly influence behavior, relationships, and our capacity for expansion. The Records show us that shame is energetic. It can be passed on, embedded, and even mistaken for identity. But once brought into conscious awareness, it can be seen for what it is: an illusion created by separation from our Divine knowing. And from this space of awareness, we are invited to release it completely.

M: Why am I continually involved in a struggle for power among some of my colleagues and friends? I'm referring to their disappearing when it's time to step up to the plate and continue toward success.

AR: You are right in what you are thinking. Each one who does not follow through is afraid of success when they are at its door. You are not afraid of this. You have had training for so many years working in live television that, when it is time to go on the air, you have no choice but to go forward. Use this asset now. This is your nature.

M: But why have I manifested people who are afraid to move forward?

AR: Since you are aware that they are afraid to move forward, this is a sign that you have moved beyond them, because you are expanding.

M: Why am I aware of it to begin with?

AR: It is your shame that holds you back.

M: What shame is this?

AR: Shame connected to your childhood in this lifetime. Your subconscious took it on. Remember, the subconscious simply records everything that is happening when you are little. It does not judge. It just records. You have an energy of shame that is part of your family lineage. They lived with it, and the energy of their perception of their shame was recorded onto your subconscious. And, as your quantum teachers express today, your subconscious runs over ninety percent of your behavior from the background. Your conscious is not aware of this, in your case, shame, until you bring it forward through intended awareness.

M: So, I absorbed this shame from my family?

AR: Not absorbed, simply recorded. With awareness, you can unlink yourself from the (perceived) shame to discover your true nature, which is God/Source.

Let us exchange more about this human-created—actually, ego-created—idea, which is shame. When a person thinks about their actions, at first it is just that—simple thoughts or a remembering of exactly what occurred and what things that person did during those circumstances. Now, once the remembering is complete, meaning you have no more thoughts about those actions, there remains this pivotal space. You can move on with no judgment, or while in this space—depending on whether you are tapped into your Divine light—the ego can slide in and join your mind to create interpretations and new thoughts of low self-worth, which can then be reflected back to you as an emotion, and that emotion can form into what you refer to as shame.

M: I can see how that can grow into shame. But what if we cannot remember moments, such as past lives or subconscious patterns that we are not yet aware of?

AR: If those memories are, in a sense, buried in your subconscious or if you have not yet remembered a past life, the energy of those memories still exists in you, and your perspectives (from the time the actions happened) will be attached to them. Were you clear about those actions? Or did you choose shame about them? Your perspectives from those lifetimes and those that lie within your subconscious are still connected with those times or those actions and can remain with you in your present lifetime.

M: So, this can be a block? Can you give an example of this?

AR: Yes. As an example, a man in his present lifetime may be confused as to why he cannot manifest success in his life. He then may discover that he lived as a leader in a past lifetime, that he led people in what he believed was the right path, yet he may have caused harm or even death for some because of the path he chose for all of them. Most likely, somewhere along his soul's journey, he interpreted his actions, and when remembering them—in that lifetime or a later one—he chose thoughts of low self-worth (shame). Instead of looking at his actions as simply actions taken in the name of God/Source or light, when he was remembering them, an ego-conscious energy of low worth may have entered his consciousness in the form of shame. That shame is not necessarily connected to his actions, but rather to his perception of those actions. And the energy of that shame will follow along with him from lifetime to lifetime, until he can separate the two and see his original actions as just what they were (without the negative perceptions about them). Also, when you allow negative perceptions in the form of shame to be created, the energy of those perceptions (low self-worth, which is NEVER who you are) will be recognized by others around you who are in that same low vibratory state, and they will help make your shame real. To leap over to you, Mary, as another example of this: in one of your lifetimes, when you experienced scorn, others around you grabbed on to it and hurled it back to you—in a sense, to validate it for you. You had the feeling of scorn first, then it was recognized and validated by those of the same vibration. That is why you experienced being scorned by others. We are not referring to how you scorned others through your actions. We are merely trying to create an understanding about how (perceived) shame can form itself.

M: But what about those original actions, especially those that cause harm to others? It feels wrong to say they are simply actions. If someone kills another, it seems too simple to refer to the killing as just an action.

AR: When you look at everything as energy, which everything is, it is just that—energy transferred into an action. What you, as humans, do about these actions can evolve into uncertainty and pain, which there seems to be much of on your planet at this period in your history. We are not condoning actions that harm others. Actions that harm others are (in themselves) non-Divine. Again, we will emphasize the power of the (non-existent!) ego. Non-Divine space can become a target for non-Divine actions, set up and created by the ego.

M: So, how can we release any shame that we may have taken on in this or past lifetimes?

AR: The most important first step is to be aware that you may have taken on shame to begin with. This will happen when you remember your past or your present childhood. It is easy in your present psychology to look back and put the responsibility for your pain or suffering onto others. The ego loves this because it keeps you in victimhood. There is no such thing as victimhood. Try to remember these events (from your consciousness) as just events, with no thing attached to them, as if you were viewing the events of someone else. This is so important. Once you separate your perceptions of those events/times, you can view them from your Divine perspective, which is what is real. You will discover that those actions made sense, meaning they made sense when and why they occurred to begin with. You do not need to justify them, but rather, understand them. This is a very subtle, powerful space to be in, and one that Divine fills. You then can experience a kind of freedom when you separate the perceptions of shame, pain, and more from the initiating events.

What also may help you in this journey is to realize that your perceived shame was never yours to begin with! So why claim something that is not yours?

Remember, ego does not want you free. It loves to create a false victimhood that can prevent you from accessing your greatness, and this can then become your (perceived) block. Once you have the awareness—the power—about how this all works and manifests, then you can use this power to harness the energy around those original actions (without the negative perceptions) as a powerful tool for Divine expansion and self-love. More loving, honorable, not fear-based people will show up in your life, and you will experience joy—pure joy.

Through this Akashic exchange, I was gently led into a deeper understanding of myself and shame. The Akashic Realm offers us this truth: we are not designed to take on or to carry a burden that was never ours to begin with. We are not meant to be diminished by what the egoic mind has falsely defined as failure turned into shame. Instead, we are invited to step back into our Divine essence, to transmute perceived shame into power, compassion, and joy. That is true alchemy and the path of remembering who we really are.

FEAR

I'VE LIVED A GOOD PART of my life believing that fear was something real—something to overcome, manage, or work through. I opened my Akashic Records in this session not with a specific concern but with a subtle feeling—a lingering vibration I could not name, a heaviness that did not feel like mine. I asked the Records about it. What followed unraveled everything I thought I knew about fear. This was not just a gentle reminder about choosing love. It was a complete reframing of fear's existence, or rather, its nonexistence.

M: Lately, I have been feeling a kind of unease or anxiousness, but I cannot quite place what is causing it. Is this fear? And if so, where is it coming from?

AR: Fear does not exist. Your world has singled it out as a condition that not only exists but that needs to be harnessed, transmuted, figured out, manipulated, and more. Fear is that moment of perception when a human being or a collective of human beings stops to observe an event or condition from a place of non-love. It is the perception of fear that has created it, and again, we emphasize that it emerges (falsely) from the ego. You see, the ego wants you all to feed it. This is how it remains as what it perceives as relevant.

Let us look at a life without this perceived fear. Mother Teresa lived without fear. How? She lived love only. She did not stop to contemplate her actions when she placed herself in the midst of what you all would refer to as the "very sick" or "ill." She trusted; she knew that love is the one true power. Many around her witnessed what they would term her fortitude and often tried to dissuade her from walking among the sick. They claimed to be fearful for her, but in reality, they were experiencing their own fear. And due to this fear, they placed her on a pedestal, for they perceived that her not being in fear was something miraculous.

Mother Teresa did not wish to be idolized. It made no sense to her, as she was merely living in the Divine essence of love itself! The same is true of Gandhi and all lightworkers on Earth. They are living and acting on the deep understanding of the power of love, of kindness. They know no fear.

We also want to pose some differentiations here. There are things such as hesitancy, apprehension, perceived inaction, and observation. Let us shine a light on these, as they often become entangled with this idea of the existence of fear. Apprehension and hesitancy, when fueled by love, are powerful actions (yes, actions!) that, when balanced in love itself, become wonderful elements of strategy and living life.

Let us look at the (perceived) death of a loved one. Quite often, when someone loses a loved one, what can occur is the development of a state of fear, which often is this person's fear of their own death or demise and may be a sign that the ego has slipped in to make itself relevant.

However, they can choose to reflect on their deceased from the space of love. They can stand—in these first moments of realization that the loved one is no longer existing on the Earth plane—in a space of Universal acknowledgment of the unending light of that loved one. We are not implying that there may not be tears and sadness. But when the sadness or tears can breathe love itself into the love that the deceased was and is, this will have a profound and beautiful effect on the one who is experiencing this perceived loss. Ultimately, this raised vibration will result in the expansion of the experiencer. Everything feeds into Source, for Source is love. And, of course, there is no loss because there is no death.

The Ancients did not recognize fear. They met life head-on, moment to moment. When life places something in front of you, and when you take immediate action from your intuitive centers, there is no time for fear to be created. Fear manifests when you stop in front of what comes up in your life and think on it. The ego loves this. A pocket of uncertainty arises, and the energy of fear appears.

Fear appears from separation from Divine. When you know you are Divine light, you will know (without even thinking on it) that all is well. Fear cannot live or be created from that space of all is well.

Separation from our inner Divinity sets up a place that ego loves. It slips in and tries to run the show, often wreaking havoc as it does. But remember, the ego and fear are non-existent. Ego tricks humans into thinking they are in control of their lives. True control of a human life emerges from the knowing that you are the Divine light of God/Source.

M: What is inner Divinity?

AR: Knowing you are love, joy, and that you are complete.

To be told that fear does not exist felt shocking at first. But as I sat with it, deeply, I began to feel its truth. Fear is not a force. It is a byproduct of forgetting who we are. It arises only in the absence of love, and it feeds only on separation from Source. I came to the understanding that the only true antidote to fear is remembering that I am Divine light—complete, whole, and eternal. And this truth is not just for me; it is for all of us. The moment we remember our inner Divinity, fear has nowhere to live. It disappears, not because we have conquered it, but because we have stopped giving it a stage on which to perform.

LETTING GO

ETTING GO HAS always sounded simpler than it feels. For years, it meant effort—doing something, releasing something, fixing something. But when I brought this to my Akashic Records, I was shown something quite different. Letting go is not about what we do—it's about what we stop doing. It is a return to stillness, to neutrality, to presence—and in that space, we can finally experience the Divine. This reading gave me a whole new framework for surrender—one that is practical, honest, and entirely possible.

M: What does that moment of letting go and allowing Divine to run the show look and feel like?

AR: It will feel like a tiny moment of no resistance, no worry. It will feel like you are doing nothing at all. Then it will be immediately followed by a desire to take an action. The mind cannot interfere at this time because you have now entered a space of no interference. Then Divine takes over. Once Divine takes over, magnificently, the ego cannot play or have its way. This creates a portal directly connected to your soul, its desires, and its role in this lifetime. When you are moved into this space of light, the juice of the ethers can flow through to you like a gushing waterfall. And you get to play in it. You can experience any or all of it and transfer it through your God-given tools of training, skills, and expertise. Earth does this amazingly and unendingly well. It is how the plants and trees transform and rejuvenate, how your land and ocean animals move about. Even your human cells allow the electric light of their Divine to run the show. Your cells simply go for the ride. And they are in constant joy over and through it all!

M: Wow. This is so beautiful!

AR: Yes, it is, Mary. The more you access your Akashic Records and this Divine space of no time, of nothingness, which really means everything-ness, the more aligned you will be to your chosen path in this lifetime. And when that happens, all past patterns that do not serve this journey simply dissolve away or transform back to the light.

M: So, we do not need to work on dissolving past negative patterns?

AR: Those patterns have never been negative. They were simply chosen actions and experiences that related to and pertained to that time. They have become interpreted by your present you as negative because of the ego's attachment to judgment. So, you see, if these patterns were never bad to begin with, then there is no reason to even be considering them today. They are simply a dimension of the fabric of each human soul. When you take this in, you can experience more wholeness as a human being. So, to answer your question, there is no need to work on dissolving past patterns. Ego will try to implant negative interpretations of the past as a means to distract you from your Divine center of living and wellness. Life becomes so much easier and joyful from this perspective, yes?

M: Absolutely! I can feel ease right now as I receive this. Thank you.

AR: Yes, so go about today allowing those moments, like the one this morning. And keep asking the Spirit of light to run your show, then simply follow the signs and inspirations for action. Ask the Holy Spirit of light to take charge today!

Since receiving this, I've begun noticing small moments when I stop *efforting*—and a quiet ease arrives. That is the shift. That is the space where the Divine starts running the show. It is not dramatic. It is not even always noticeable. But it is real. The more I allow it, the more I see how much of my life can move forward without me pushing. Letting go is not about escaping the past or fixing what is broken. It's about realizing nothing ever was broken. And from that place, I can finally live.

THE CONCEPT OF WORRY

THIS AKASHIC EXCHANGE began with a simple feeling—disconnection. I woke up that morning feeling out of alignment with a project I had previously been excited about, and I noticed a familiar undercurrent of worry sneaking in. Later that same day, my wife made a comment about worry, and I knew it was surfacing for a reason. When I opened my Akashic Records, what unfolded was one of the clearest explanations I have ever received about the nature of worry, its connection to ego, and why it continues to hold so many of us back from peace. What I learned shifted something fundamental in how I understand the energy of worry—and how I can choose not to feed into it.

M: As I awoke this morning, I had this feeling of not being connected to the television series I had been writing. It was as if I could just walk away from the project, and it would not matter. Then I thought about what my wife, Christine, had mentioned yesterday about worry. What was that for me?

AR: Yes, indeed. Worry is a common one on planet Earth. You see, it lives in the ego's world. The ego generates and commands several major emotions in humans. Worry is one of its powerful ones. And remember that since the ego is not real, then worry is not either.

M: I noticed this morning that as I became aware of the negative feeling about my television series, it slowly became replaced with a sense of looking forward to working on it today.

AR: Part of what happened was you were not entirely awake yet. As you began to come back from deep sleep, the ego began to, in a sense, wake up, too. But the real part of you—the part that always knows that all is well—was still in charge. So, it encouraged an automatic shift into light, and you began to think about opening the Akashic Records of the series itself. And then the other negative feeling dissipated—yes?

M: That is exactly what happened. I was also aware of the disappearance of the negative thought. It was strange to have it be my experience, while I was observing it shift at the same time.

AR: Yes. This is why you are a good writer, Mary. You are the experiences you are writing about, and you can jump in and out of them from varying perspectives. It is a gift.

M: I am seeing it in a new way. I would like to know more about the energy of worry and why it's so prevalent on our planet today.

AR: Worry is an energy whose purpose is to dismantle humans from their Divine centers. And that it does. Or we should emphasize that this is what humans choose to step into—this worry energy. There appears to be discomfort among humans with the concept that all is well. This discomfort appeared when the ego became recognized. Ego searches for dissent and negativity as a way to keep itself relevant.

M: Isn't this ego energy needed as a way to create contrast, so that we can experience the joy of "all is well"?

AR: That is one belief and a validation for the existence of ego. But this perception was born from ego itself! There is never a need for contrast. Joy and love on their own are powerful, everlasting tools for life—always.

When there is a sensation of all is well, you enter into a space of calm, centered nothingness. That is how it feels, yes? And then your mind (ego) steps in to save you from the nothingness, as if it is a bad thing. However, nothingness is a powerful state where humans and God/Source can play, converse, and dance. It is where powerful light exchanges happen, ideas and creativity for humanity are birthed, multi-dimensions are experienced and explored. It is the space for ultimate expansion. Worry crushes this space with its dense energy. When this occurs, you become aware of this difference between the two, and you call it contrast. To call it contrast is to validate ego's existence, do you see? The word contrast itself implies two things of equal but opposite quality. Ego will never be of equal quality to joy and love. It cannot because it is not real!

So, when you experience thoughts or feelings of worry, take a moment (as you did this morning) to look at it as it is coming into your mind/body. Observe it. Then ask yourself if the worry is justified. In that moment of observation, you will experience that there is never anything to worry about. Worry is crafted from the negative what-ifs of the ego.

Self-doubt is at the heart of the ego. (Yes, the ego thinks it has a heart!) Self-doubt sets up shop in an individual sometimes without the individual participating! By this, we mean that the individual has not yet developed intelligence or is in a non-loving environment. Ego uses these circumstances to gain a foothold. In humans who are also experiencing their inner light, it will be a battle. But we want you to see that there does not need to ever be a battle. The perception of your Earth today is that it is in a state of chaos. That could not be further from the truth. Yes, there are imbalances, mishaps, and what you call mistakes, but these pale in comparison to what the light is doing.

Each one of you is love. And each one of you has the God-given right to joy, love, and happiness, all the time. That is the law! You are already light! When you feel and know it inside, you will have fewer opportunities to worry. You will get to a space where there is never worry of any kind.

Some will say, "But sometimes when I worry about something, I find out that there was a justified reason to worry." When you have this idea, you send out a Universal request to prove it to yourself. So, you look for it, and bam, it shows up for you. This is not proof. This is manifestation. Worry by itself cannot stand alone. It needs perceptions of it to live, and it needs attention on it to survive.

There is never a justification for worry. Because the natural state of everything is that all is well . . . all the time. That is it!

We suggest that you play around with the idea of worry. Try not to feed into it, but from this Divine perspective here, develop an awareness of when it shows up in your thinking. Challenge the actual worry in that exact moment. You will catch it almost not knowing what it, itself, is! It will stare back at you frozen as it looks for proof of its existence. But it will not be able to bring it forward. If you join hands with it, you both will walk a path of nonexistent distractions from who you really are. So, it is in this small moment of its arrival that you can direct your deep attentions back to your light. The more you exercise this, the less you will experience worry, and your world will begin to fill up with everything and everyone who celebrates joy, light, and love . . . Always.

M: This is so good. Thank you.

AR: We will be exchanging with you more on this topic, as the ego could be a book in itself, but of course, the ego would want that, wouldn't it?

M: Will there ever be a time when there is no ego?

AR: Yes. And it will be (as it was at the birth of planet Earth)—when humankind stops seeing itself and simply experiences (from one individual to the next) the purity of its Divineness. We wish for you to experience the love you are, not to see yourselves outside of it. The greatest gift that humans can give themselves is to lose their reflection. Only love will exist then.

This exchange reminded me that worry is not truth. It is not even helpful. It is just an energy that thrives on attention and survives through habit. And when I observe it closely, it dissolves, because it was never real to begin with.

The Akashic Records showed me that I do not need to fight worry. I just need to recognize that it does not belong to my Divine self. It is a trick of the ego—clever, persistent, but ultimately powerless in the presence of awareness. When we meet worry not with resistance but with light, peace becomes the default—not the exception. And from that place we can finally trust that all is well . . . always.

THE POWER OF TRAUMA

I'VE OFTEN WRESTLED with the weight of trauma—my own, that of those close to me, and the collective stories that I've encountered in my work. Trauma can feel so final, so consuming, that it is easy to believe it defines who we are. When I brought this into my Akashic Records, I was met not with judgment or explanation, but with a shift in perception—one that reframed trauma not as a wound to carry, but as an energy that can be mined and transmuted into power. I was not being asked to diminish what happened, but to expand how I see it. What if our most painful moments hold the very key to the light we came here to live?

M: I want to exchange about the ideas surrounding trauma. It seems to be such a prevalent barrier for people to move forward in their lives.

Divine often talks about "mining the energy" of past trauma. What does this mean?

AR: Humans often refer to events in their lives and the memories of said events as traumatic. If you all could see that this is a dangerous perception that keeps humans in victimhood. We are not diminishing the effects that some perceived trauma has had on humanity. But we would like to offer a different way of perceiving trauma.

Events that hurt you or make you feel bad are always part of your soul's journey. This is hard for some to grasp because humans then wonder how they would have created negative events in their lives.

Let us look at the energy of trauma. The power of trauma lies in its energy.

M: Can you give an example of this?

AR: Yes. Let us look at a child who has been abused in some way. That child's soul did not choose to incarnate specifically to be abused. That is never a soul's choice. But the soul of that child may have chosen to experience life events that are part of that child's soul journey later in life. Or the choice to be in an abusive family may also be a way for that child to become a beacon of love. Because, by choosing a household of non-love, the child will ricochet into her life on a massive love quest. And by sharing with others her childhood experiences, those others get to choose expansion through compassion and love. It is a remarkable choice when a soul enters a lifetime to experience extremes in energies. This is what (perceived) trauma is. It is an extreme energy of un-love. Now, because it is energy, it is neither good nor bad, until it is interpreted or perceived.

When you visit the Akashic Records around perceived trauma, we encourage you to look at those events from a non-perspective or non-opinionated space. This is, in no way, an attempt to justify the conditions of the trauma. Instead, we suggest that you identify the energy of the events. Further, if a child—now an adult—is remembering childhood events as trauma, their Akashic Records, as a direct mirror of their Divinity, can help transmute that trauma energy into power.

M: What might this look like?

AR: So, in the case of a person who was beaten as a child, we can lovingly look at these events. Once in their Akashic Records, their Divine will shower light onto the events. We might ask specifically how that person felt before the events or immediately after. Most of the time, when someone is being abused in some way, it initiates a power in that person. That power is the passion to stop it, a desire to get away, a desire to speak their truth. And since they are being prevented from any of that, it ramps up their desires. This is why so many humans who have had tough or traumatic beginnings go on to do remarkable things! They become teachers, healers, inventors, and imaginators!

These events also affect others around the child or person experiencing the perceived trauma. Organizations have been formed, books written, lawyers have fought for rights, films produced, and laws enacted, all in dedication and pursuit of changing these events into positive energy. That immense focus on transforming the trauma into power brings masses of people together in love and light. There is so much that emanates from perceived trauma.

M: This is sounding like trauma is a good thing.

AR: No, it is neither good nor bad. For the perpetrators, it is when they know not that they are Divine beings of God/Source, and they allow their egos to run everything, that they choose these unloving actions. A soul who chooses to be part of this ego manifestation is either releasing past-life energies related to the ego or they are learning about self-love. Those who are the receivers of this un-Divineness are always molding that negative energy into light in some way, even if that individual dies in the process. Look at what happens on your planet if a child dies at the hands of an empty person (perpetrator). The love that emanates from the event creates such expansion that you would be blinded by it if you could see it! This is what the soul of Jesus chose to do! His soul chose to incarnate and live love at a dangerous and dark time in history. The contrast between what Jesus lived and what people during his time believed was right is what has transmuted into love on every level. Observe how Jesus and his teachings still power the planet! It is pure Christ Consciousness.

We would like to honor every person on Earth who chooses to enter into difficult situations and experiences. When we exchange within someone's Akashic Records about the gift that is the perceived trauma, and we reflect to them the immense light that they were before the trauma and still are at every present moment, and when we impart to them that they have chosen this gift, then the trauma transforms itself into power—into opportunities that enable a person to live their soul's chosen journey more powerfully.

More specifically, a child who was physically abused learns resistant energy. Resistance can be a powerful tool in life when certain obstacles arise. Or a child who was not valued for their voice or opinion—through the energy of being unable to express—craves expression throughout their lifetime. Because of the nature of having been shut down at an early age, they will passionately seek and express it in a stronger way, by powering past and out from the energy of not having a voice.

This is how you can "mine" past experiences for the opportunities they present to you in life. It takes courage for individuals to go on this journey, but when the journey takes place within your Akashic Records, it is never difficult. Our process serves as a living reminder and expression of the Divine love inherent in each of you. And remember that when you are in your Akashic Records, you are dialoguing with the Divine aspect of you. As your Masters, Teachers, and Loved Ones, we are the light energies guiding you to experience the love that is you and, in turn, encouraging you to live your chosen path.

M: How does the idea of sacrifice relate to trauma? Is the soul choosing sacrifice when that soul reincarnates into a dire situation, such as physical, mental, or sexual abuse?

AR: We want to remind you all that the soul is not choosing the specifics of its life. The soul chooses the essence, the ideas that it will take part in, in support of its chosen overarching path. Events that you refer to as horrific are choices in the moment, always connected to your soul's journey. There are no mistakes . . . ever. This is a hard one for humans to let in, often because they have become attached to the third-dimensional, dramatic perspectives surrounding their perceived trauma. Once a person opens up to expand those perspectives, a new human emerges. Then that individual can step outside their trauma and look at it in terms of their soul's journey on the planet at a specific time in history.

Now, sacrifice is another term that we would like to clarify. The term sacrifice imposes another man-made perception that has nothing to do with love. Humankind has equated sacrifice with love. Sacrifice implies that you are willingly giving something up (no matter how much pain and suffering it may cause) to make a point about an idea or cause. Sacrifice implies victimhood. Can you all feel into this? It is also entirely ego-based! Those who choose sacrifice are also choosing to be seen for what they are doing. Jesus Christ has been given the term sacrifice for what he did at the end of his life. This could not be further from the truth! Rather, Jesus chose to incarnate to live as a representative of unconditional love. He did not agree to die on the cross (specifically) before coming back to this planet. Oh yes—Jesus was here long before your recorded history shows him here! He made a soul agreement to live and spread love, no matter what the present moments in his life presented to him. His legacy has become misinterpreted as sacrifice, which then mistakenly holds him up high and out of reach to individuals. Religions have participated in and often created this story. Jesus did not teach that he or anyone else should be held high. He taught the exact opposite. Every human being, every living organism right down to atoms, is a living, breathing entity—a direct mirror—of God/Source. The ego has concocted the idea of sacrifice to create separation from Divine. Think about how people view someone who has supposedly sacrificed themselves for an idea or cause. They erect statues in their name, they paint portraits of them, they write volumes on that person's life that otherwise would not have been done if not for the creation of sacrifice. We see a planet where there is no need for this idea. The idea of sacrifice also implies that to create peace and love, one must give up something, and often that something is a human life. This is not Divine truth. The decision to crucify Jesus was as much an expression of the souls' chosen paths who made that decision as it was Jesus' path to stand up for love. They were opposing ideas at the time, and interestingly enough, both sides, in a sense, won. Those authority figures who joined in the belief that Jesus' ideas were a threat were in line with their souls' chosen journeys! They were taking part in shining a light on love through their actions. The events surrounding Jesus' crucifixion have spiralled out onto your planet in a blanket of love and compassion never before experienced! Was it because of sacrifice? Not at all. It was because of choice! Also, those individuals who took part in the crucifixion of Jesus have been back on the planet many times in bodies that have carried out the most amazing things in your times. They were able to garner the energy of their times, which opposed the teachings of Jesus and God/Source and transmute that energy into light and love. They could not do this without their past-life experiences of un-love.

Another interesting thing for you to hear—negative energy and positive energy are the same thing! They are energy. Period. The positive or negative is simply an interpretation of the same energy.

This is how you can transmute past perceived trauma. Trauma also implies that you have become a victim of your circumstances. However, every event, every circumstance, is always in some way aligned and related to your soul's path.

Every human being, every living organism, is a direct mirror of God/Source. This Source is at the center of everything. How you experience Source is reflected and expressed through the choices and events of your lives. When humankind separates from the knowledge that it is Divine, ego can enter the picture (yet again!), and it can create misinterpretations of these events that set up individuals to feel and express themselves as less than love.

This exchange helped me understand that trauma, in the Akashic sense, is not a permanent scar. It is an energy that is always part of our soul's chosen journey as it awaits transformation. Within the Records, I have seen how even the darkest human experiences can become conduits for Divine love. This is not about bypassing pain, but about viewing it through a broader lens, one that sees every event as part of each soul's chosen path. When we release our attachment to the victim story and open to the deeper truth, something extraordinary happens. We return to our original light. And from that place, our lives and the world begin to heal.

TOUCH

ONE MORNING AS I was waking, the word *touch* landed in my awareness—clear and certain. As I sat with it, the concept unfolded—not just a word but a knowing, a frequency, a call to remember something we are on the brink of forgetting. We are living in a time when physical contact is fading from daily life, replaced by fear and sterilized distance. I brought this into my Akashic Records, and what came forward was a powerful reminder of the sacred nature of touch—how even the briefest moment of contact between two human beings creates a vibratory expansion of love that travels far beyond what we can see. I was reminded that vibration is the language of the cosmos, and *touch* is one of its purest expressions.

M: I'm exchanging over an idea—a word first—that came to me this morning as I awoke. The word is *touch*.

AR: Humans are touching much less today than ever before in your history. Think of it. Even the change you get from a cashier in the grocery stores most often comes through a chute into a round end where you scoop up your change.

At some smaller stores, when a cashier is about to hand you your change, they place the bill in your hand first, then the change on top of the bill, never making contact with your hand.

Humans are not allowed to physically touch the food in stores and restaurants, and they wear gloves for that purpose.

M: Why have we come to this?

AR: Because humanity has been lied to over and over as your human years advance. The idea of touch, or physical connection, has been determined to be harmful to you. The idea that disease and bacteria are transmitted this way is so not true. This is another distraction in your third dimension from raising your vibrations.

Touch, and the resulting changes when touch occurs, are amazing. When two vibrating beings touch, if even for a split second, an interchange happens. Both vibrations merge in an instant, creating a newer, higher vibration that feeds into the Universe. Sometimes it is recognized by the individuals who have touched, and sometimes it is not, depending on whether they are in their ego state. But even if they are in their ego state, this exchange, no matter how small, creates this amazing wave of combined vibration.

M: Why doesn't the ego state taint the vibrations?

AR: Because ego is not real. It is a manufactured realization of humans. What is real is vibration. Vibration does not know ego. Vibration is all-knowing unto itself. It is an energy field that runs through humanity into the Universe. The design of vibration is to expand into eternity and beyond.

M: How was vibration initially formed?

AR: It was never formed. It always existed. But it could not grow unless it became engaged or recognized in some way. In other words, without it being used, it stayed the same. Then, when humanity appeared, the two met, and throughout history, man and vibration have been in a dance. Vibration flows through and around humans—physically, mentally, and imaginarily. It is all vibration. And when this merging occurs, there is always a positive result.

M: But isn't there sometimes a negative result?

AR: There is never a negative result. If there is a feeling of negativity, it is because the human being is perceiving it as negative, most likely from a place of discomfort within themselves. Energy exchange equals power.

Of course, when there is a perceived sense of love around these vibratory exchanges, they emanate out into the Universe in a much grander way. This is because love is the leader of all that is.

Let us explain further. Love is why the cosmos exists. Everything, everywhere, including the idea of infinity, is held by love and was birthed by love. This is an immense concept for humans to understand, but this is the truth of the Universe. Vibrations and energy are tools for love. When they are engaged in the name of love, the Universe expands, the energy expands and grows, and love experiences itself, and it expands even more and in turn feeds back into the cosmos.

M: Will this cycle ever end? Will love ever become . . . over?

AR: Never. In this time of perceived chaos on your planet, we encourage humans to use the tools of vibratory energy exchange, even in the tiniest (again, perceived) ways.

Another phenomenon (your word) that occurs when touch happens—when the event starts, no matter what kind of touch it is—is that this vibratory and perceived minuscule moment grows in place and spins out into the Universe. It is immediate. As it does, it circles through those engaged in the touch, as the combination of the various vibrations, no matter whether two or more individuals are involved. Depending on where each individual is in their journey, some will greatly experience the exchange, and some will not. But you must know this: for even those who are not perceiving the exchange, it is still happening for them. They may sense it later in life or may unknowingly touch (metaphorically or actually) someone else. And when they do touch another, they will have a sense that they do not know where it came from in them. Oftentimes, they may even state this.

M: So why did this come to me this morning?

AR: You are a writer, Mary. We will emphasize this to you. As we have shared in various exchanges, when you take on this "task" (perceived), we will assist you in such ways that writing will become the easiest thing you have ever engaged in during this lifetime.

You have done more than you need in terms of research, keeping an eye on what kinds of storytelling seem to have wonderful effects on viewers and audiences. No further work is needed. Please let this concept into your being, Mary. Your ego has been running the show more than you realize. Reread this reading. Trust in your inner knowing. It is from that place that you will write with ease, fun, and grace.

Regarding touch, this is a much-needed idea right now, and one that will awaken people to their inner potential. It will re-untie them from the bounds of their ego-conceived unloving lives. You are being given this now as you are awakening more and more from your ego-sleep.

M: This is amazing and so powerful for me to hear.

AR: Yes, we know this, Mary. Let us leap with love into the untying of humanity from its perceived bindings.

It is why you have chosen to be here at this time, and why you are coming into contact with those with whom you are meant to connect.

What I received from the Records affirmed what I've always sensed: Touch is not merely physical—it is vibrational, energetic, and deeply sacred. Even in a single fleeting moment, touch generates waves of light that ripple through the Universe. Whether we are aware of it or not, we affect one another with every exchange. Touch reminds us that we are not separate—we are part of a greater dance of energy, fueled by love, expanding through vibration. In a world where we are taught to fear contact, we must remember that it is in our reaching out, in our connection, that we awaken. This message, given to me through the Records, is for all of us.

EATING, ENERGY, AND THE RETURN TO DIVINE BALANCE

For a long time, I quietly struggled with the idea of consuming meat, chicken, and fish. It wasn't about health, though we now know much more about the benefits of plant-based diets, but rather about something deeper. The more I learned about how these animals arrive on our plates, the more I felt a pain I could not ignore. The word "slaughter" echoed in my mind—not just as a process, but as a reflection of our disconnection from these gorgeous living beings we share our planet with.

I turned to the Akashic Records to find clarity. What unfolded surprised me. The guidance I received gently reframed my understanding of animal life, choice, and soul purpose, which opened into a multidimensional conversation about consciousness, energy, and the very nature of nourishment itself.

M: I feel bad about taking the life of another living being. It feels wrong to me deep inside.

AR: This is your mind, Mary. The emotion you experience around what is happening to the animals who have come to feed and nurture you is coming from your mind. We can assure you that these heavenly creatures are not suffering in the way you all view that word and its meaning. There is no suffering during transitioning. They are here to nurture and teach mankind so many things. Those who are part of what you refer to as slaughter are playing a huge role on your planet. They will bring humanity back to love. Of course, you do not really need to eat animal protein. Your planet has even more to offer than you have discovered in terms of food and nourishment.

M: But what about the unloving way that humanity is treating these animals? This cannot be love. We have lost respect for the choice animals are making to nurture us.

AR: Indeed, yes, there has been a change on your planet about this all. We will offer more clarity around this issue as it may be very needed at this time in your history. Each animal soul enters a lifetime with a role, just as every human does. Not every animal soul chooses slaughter. The word slaughter evolved from the non-love that you speak of. It is more of a disconnection from God/Source that each human who participates in it is acting from. When we stated earlier that the animals are not suffering, what we mean is that on a deep soul level, they know this is why they are here. The suffering you refer to is more of a dis-ease about how they are being allowed to transition. And, Mary, remember that you are in your Akashic Records at this moment. We are reflecting to you your history, your imprints, as they pertain to your present lifetime. One of your past lifetimes involved the killing of animals for sustenance. And in that lifetime, there was a respect and honoring of the animal during the process. Your being upset about how this is handled today may be more pronounced because the way animals are being killed is missing the respect, the love, the appreciation that was part of your life so many lifetimes ago.

M: But help me understand that they may not be suffering.

AR: We can offer a good example in your lifetime. On the day of your 9/11 event, when so many thousands of people transitioned, if you look at it as an event of violence where those individuals became victims of it, this thought is exactly that . . . a thought. The truth is this: The soul of each of those thousands who transitioned that day, chose, on a soul level, to participate in one of the grandest designs of love on your planet. There was not one person across your world who did not become involved in some way in that event. People came together without a single thought about their differences. This is love. We are not diminishing the physical experiences of those people who transitioned that day. But it was not suffering, as you refer to suffering. When you hold on to the idea of suffering, you bypass the deeper Divine law that is this: Everything not only has a purpose but has choice. And, to bring it back to your animal kingdom, those animal souls who are, in a sense, participating in slaughter, are, on a deeper level, taking part in another grand design of love. They are more powerful and more in charge than you realize. We hope you can feel into this. When your mind/emotions turn in place with the idea of suffering (your perception of it), you remain in a place of acceptance of that perceived suffering. Do you see? However, when you can step outside this circle, you can then see the design, and only then can you take part in the transformation of these unloving actions into actions of love and respect for all living creatures. The animals' role in all of this is to guide you, as a humanity, back to God/Source, to love.

M: Wow. Will there be a time when humans do not need to eat food the way we do now?

AR: We assure you that there was a time when food as you know it today did not exist. Beings existed and were fed and sustained entirely by love and compassion, and from the energy of the planets, the sun, and the moon. Imagine this, Mary, as we know you are beginning to understand. Go there now with us to remember this time.

M: Is it what the Arcturian ET race has shared?

AR: Yes, and many more nonphysical races like the Arcturians. The love and compassion that was exchanged was more than enough to sustain life. And it provided the energy to power their worlds as well. The energy field around love is one your scientists have not tapped into yet, but they will. We are speaking of the field around love, not around your heart, which we realize is being measured in your world currently. Your human race forgot about the power behind love.

M: Why did it change?

AR: Ego. Once humans saw themselves outside of love, outside of themselves, they began to interpret its value, which love does not know. Love started to become a forgotten thing, and humans discovered other ways to nurture themselves, so they turned to their planet and to each other. When your planet once again understands and practices the idea that love can fulfill everything, it will begin to come back into balance.

M: Is this why we are depleting our food sources by polluting them and fighting over them?

AR: Absolutely. It is moving along according to a plan that was mapped out way before you arrived here. For love to become restored to its true power, all perceptions of it will have to die. Do you understand? It is the perception of love that is depleting the God-given resources around your planet. Love cannot be perceived, only experienced. Throughout your past, races or beings received and experienced love. They did not think about it, talk about it, write about it, or stare at it. It just was.

Love nurtured beings immediately, so there was never a need for food. Love was the food. Therefore, bodies were differently constructed, too, which is why beings were immortal. You have been dancing around this concept for some time, Mary. We can tell you right now that you are correct. You received that information in a flash, did you not?

M: Yes. I remember it was in a flash.

AR: Exactly, that minuscule moment was from the realms of truth. Your physical stature was sturdy and balanced . . . powerful and supple too. These races had such a love of nature that they would have never even conceived of disrupting the balance of it by consuming it. Consumption is the energy of the third dimension. It will end as you know it. Humans are fearful of this idea, which is why they keep toying with food and food sources. You do not need food and will realize that without food as you know it, you will rediscover yourselves and experience a kind of love that you cannot even imagine.

M: Wow. I have been sensing this in flashes. So, is my return to eating animal protein good or bad for me?

AR: It is as you wish. We suggested this to propel you back through time. Your remembering your past lives is part of your future here and now. You have been feeling a sense that consuming animal protein is not quite what you thought, yes?

M: Yes. It is confusing me.

AR: It is confusing you because you know on a soul level that food is not necessary. So, we suggest that you not worry about it. Eat what you sense during the minuscule flashes we are speaking of. Try it.

M: Last night, I remember having a flash of wanting the vegan food that Christine was preparing. I thought to myself, *but don't I want meat?* And it was a short moment of, *no, I want this right now.* And when I ate the vegan meal, it was fabulous and nurturing to me.

AR: That is the window we are speaking of. Listen carefully to these moments. It will help you align yourself with the fifth dimension and beyond.

Since shifting to organic fruits, vegetables, and grains, I have noticed a profound expansion in my connection to the Akashic Records. Often, I receive messages from the Divine Realm without even needing to open the Records. I know this is related to what I consume. Whole foods carry a high and vibrant frequency that mirrors the Divine.

I remember hearing fitness coach Jack LaLanne say that he didn't eat anything touched by man—and I understand that now. Today's manipulated foods have a lower natural vibration, which diminishes the life force in both the food and in us. That, in turn, weakens our immunity and makes it harder for us to handle illness.

During this reading, I also resonated with the information that, as a human race, there was a time when we didn't need to consume flesh. Throughout my life, I have noticed that I never really cared about food. I enjoyed it, yes, but I often forgot to eat, especially when I felt in joyful alignment with what I was doing. I did not suffer during those times. Now I understand why. The Records have helped me remember that we did not always eat the way we do now. Although I'm no longer personally judged for occasionally not eating, societal systems still suggest that it is unhealthy. I feel a renewed ease around this topic.

MONEY

WHO DOESN'T WANT to talk about money? It is one of the most persistent focuses in our world. I have had my struggles with money—how to make peace with it, how to receive it, and whether it has any real meaning beyond survival. I took these questions into my Akashic Records. What came through was a reframing of the way we have been taught to think about freedom, value, and happiness. What I received challenged every belief I had about money and reminded me that what we are seeking is not money at all. It is trust. It is love.

M: I am attracted to the idea that when I have more money, I will have more freedom. Is this true, or is this a trick of my ego?

AR: Money is a manufactured concept. If you notice, it is not necessary to have money to live in love. Money is not of the love energy of Mother Earth.

M: But we cannot live without it. How do we juggle that? I am very unfamiliar with money and its role. It confuses me.

AR: Your financial well-being always came to you in past lifetimes, as a result of your role in life then—how you lived and what you did. It was the result of an "exchange" for you. This is why you have settled into jobs here that were structured around an exchange of services for financial rewards. Now that you are out from that structure, you are "floating about," not quite sure how to bring it in. Yes?

M: Yes, how can I step into a new place, where it comes in and feels right and comfortable and useful to me for my work ahead?

AR: Stop thinking about it and about money increasing your ability to accomplish things. This, too, is the ego at work. The reality is this—you and others do not need to have money to experience the joy of living and breathing love. We cannot stress this enough. Be light about money. Giggle about it, laugh at it, like you laugh at puppies. Do not rely on its existence for your happiness. Make a game out of enjoying and playing with what you have. See it as fun, and do not feed into it as a source of happiness. It is not—we guarantee. And cease figuring out how you will be bringing it to you. If you remember, not long ago, you were having fun at your work and were not even thinking about money, were you? It just kept flowing in to take care of what you needed and desired just in time, over and over again. Remember?

M: Yes. I can feel that feeling right now. It was easy, and I was never worried about money. And I always giggled when more came to me.

AR: Yes, this is the place to be in. You enjoy bubbles when you see them, yes? And you know they really do not stick around, because what they look like does not really exist. This is like money. It, too, does not stick around because it is not real. Nice metaphor for you, we feel.

Let the universal sphere of love that surrounds you take care of you. It has and always will. Always. And, as you clear up your unhealthy ways or habits, you will see only the constant flow of wellness in every aspect of your life. Everything will feel joyful and easy, and you will be having fun in a way unimaginable. Take this leap. Use your term "discipline" to line back up with who you really are. Humans are very challenged with the now. There is so much nonphysical warfare happening right now, whose energy is crossing over into your plane and causing confusion. The only way to ride this out is to become a whole, loving being, physically and spiritually.

The ego-energy wants you to see struggle, so it can continue to exist, but we will end here with this reminder—the ego does not exist.

M: What about people who have careers working in the fields of money, like bankers, stock market traders, financial consultants, CFOs, and more? Are they working with something that does not exist?

AR: Money plays a third-dimensional role in your present time period, just like your bodies do, or your various forms of nourishment. But remember, we shared that there is really no need for food. It is the same with money. You, as a humanity, have not reached that part of your Divine precipice. Those of you who are in the business of working with money, especially those who are doing it to increase their own monetary value, do not yet know that these perceptions of the value and importance of money are not real.

M: But what about if some of these people love what they are doing? They may find joy in their work. I thought if we are doing something that brings us joy, then we are aligned with our soul's path.

AR: Let us unpack these thoughts a bit. It is important to understand what kind of happiness working with and around money brings to you. Substantial amounts of money, humanity believes, will bring freedom to do and have whatever (it thinks) will bring it happiness. Freedom is not created by anything. It just is. Always. Humanity thinking that freedom must be obtained is another trick of the ego. And it is through those humans who are operating from the non-realization that they are Divine light, who are creating institutions and systems that fight to keep that idea (money is freedom) alive. But it is not real. How can you need freedom when you are already free?

You may notice in your world that as your humanity begins to expand in its own Divine light and knowledge of love, many of you are leaving the big institutions that thrive on money. And many of you are sharing how much happier you have been since. Often, you will hear stories of men and women who left their corporate, money-driven worlds to pursue creative endeavors. What happened was that their creative aspects and the powerful essence of their imaginations were becoming stifled by the untruth that money is everything. Eventually, those creative essences' desire to be realized emerged large enough to prompt a reality—love is the driving force of everything. Creativity and imagination reside within love. So, you see, something that is not real, but is believed to be real, cannot last. It eventually crumbles, or the deep love essence of you, as humans, punches through it.

M: So, how should we be thinking about and applying money in our lives? The world is set up to give, receive, and exchange money. We cannot just stop using it.

AR: Change your perception from "it rules" to the reality that "it's just a tool" in your now time. That is all that is needed. The less value (pun intended!) you give it, the easier it will flow. Money, as a tool, is best applied in your lives as a continuous ebb and flow of energy. Your oceans ebb and flow. They do not grow and take over. Weather may cause the oceans to shift and change, but the oceans stay the same. And you may say, but the beaches are eroding, so isn't the ocean doing this by becoming less? No, the oceans are co-creating with other forces for a higher purpose. Money is not in a co-creative dance like this for a higher purpose. It was created by man, and the misperceptions around it are being perpetuated by the parts of humanity that have not experienced Divine connection.

M: Will there be a time when money does not exist?

AR: Yes. Because the new Earth, which is being formed at this moment, will be one that operates completely from love. There will be no duality. It will not be needed as love has no duality. Gaia will radiate her gloriousness, and all living things will be respected and treated as equal co-creators feeding into a giant nonending well of God/Source.

This was a wonderful exchange that offered a higher vibrational attitude about money and how we are evolving as a planet. I have practiced not focusing on money, and when I do, it arrives in just the right amount and at exactly the right time to meet my needs.

Each time I reflect on this interaction, I become increasingly certain of my intrinsic worthiness and capacity for love.

CLEANSING AND TOXINS

THE FOLLOWING READING began with my need for clarification from my Akashic Records regarding the process and role of cleansing. As always, my interaction with my light energies led me down a path of amazing information and clarity, especially around the topic of humankind tampering with plants and animals and the process and meaning of extinction.

M: Since I have been on a healing cleanse, I have noticed changes, not only in my body but also in my thoughts, feelings, beliefs, etc. Why is this?

AR: Normal wear and tear from your planet begins to place layer upon layer of coverings over the essence of your human self. So, the more this happens, the more distanced you become from your powerful essence—that light that you emerged as at birth and the light that is the real you. When you begin to infuse your body with Gaia's elixirs in the form of plants, vegetables, juices, and water, the essence of Gaia finds your essence and, in a sense, begins to commune with it. This is on the physical level as well. The layers of coverings that are over your essence do not recognize Gaia. They hang around for a bit and, in some cases, balk at Gaia's intrusion, as they perceive it. Often, they put up a bit of a fight to remain in the body. This is where you see reactions that people have, such as headaches, body aches and pains, and thoughts of quitting, during a cleanse.

M: Are these the toxins we speak of in cleansing? Can you dig in further to their structure, their purpose?

AR: When humanity interferes with the natural flow of the planet and the natural flow of all living things, the energy of resistance emerges. It rises up from the natural thing being tampered with. This may be more of a "showing you who they really are." So, for example, when a plant in its natural state is changed through human manipulation, that plant will suddenly become a harmful thing to humans. We want you to realize that it is not that the plant has become a victim of its human manipulation, but rather that the essence and Divine power of that plant remains and rides through the manipulative experience of the plant right on to when it is ingested. And it will show you or call attention to itself through its effect on you as a human when you ingest it. This is nature's way of saying, "You cannot tamper with my Divinity." When you ingest this kind of plant, your body's natural essence that matches the plant's Divine essence meets up with it. But not without your essence having to maneuver its way through the plant's manipulated parts—its untruths. When your body does this, it can be challenging work and can wear a human down. This is why it may take some humans years and years of ingesting manipulated plants and vegetables or breathing bad air before one becomes depleted and often ill. Humans were meant to interact with nature on nature's Divine terms.

We want to emphasize that there is not one part of Gaia that cannot survive mankind's manipulation.

M: Why would Divine essence need to maneuver at all? If Divine essence remains in the manipulated plant, why doesn't it just cancel out the unhealthy parts of the plant, the parts that have been changed by man?

AR: Ah. Great question, Mary. Let us specifically look at one example and follow through its manipulation journey. So, let us say that a carrot is growing, unaltered in its natural, God/Source state. It literally breathes and exhales the life force of God/Source. Then, a farmer decides to add pesticide to that plant. Remember that the reason the farmer is doing this is not to kill that carrot. He is trying to prevent that carrot from being destroyed by insects and animals. This goal of the farmer is not a bad one. It is simply that he does not know the way of Divine, he is out of tune with Divine. A Divine-based solution would be to lure the other living organisms who want that carrot away, and feed them in some way, so all organisms continue to thrive. Of course, there is an even better way (from our perspective). The farmer can commune with—actually speak to—those organisms through and into the field where they exist. This field is accessible to all life on Earth, no matter what species is speaking to what species. The field is where all life exists and, therefore, can, in a sense, meet up. When the farmer speaks to those known as pests and lovingly asks them to reveal what it is they want, he will hear them. However, he must do this fully immersed in the field of Divine. It has been done.

Back to that carrot. The carrot has now been altered, so you think. However, the God/Source in that carrot can never be altered. So, someone who ingests that carrot, who acknowledges their own Divinity, will not get sick. This Divine acknowledgment will cancel out the harmful chemicals and transmute them into light. When we mentioned that the God-essence of the plant maneuvers its way through the harmful interference, we mean it rises to the top and reveals itself. The harmful substance does not stand a chance when the consumer of the carrot is knowing their Divine essence and at the same time is knowing the Divine essence of the carrot. When humans focus on the pesticide in that carrot, it enables that pesticide to see itself, and it will hang around and try harder to keep itself relevant. The pesticide does not know it is doing harm. It was created out of tune from Divine, so all it knows is to be out of tune.

M: If this transmutation happens often enough, then might that not be interpreted as the pesticides working? And more pesticides will continue to be manufactured?

AR: Yes, this is what has been happening. It is being misinterpreted by humans that they are not getting sick from the pesticides and that they are not harmful. As we have shared, when humans are more evolved, and know and experience their Divinity, that is the likely result and conclusion . . . they will not get sick. However, there are many among you, millions of people, who do not recognize this in themselves. Because they are not acknowledging their Divinity, they feed into the energy of the pesticide, empowering that pesticide to operate as it was designed . . . to kill. It does not know you are not a pest in the soil. It is on its trajectory.

The law of Divine operates from its own isness. It does not and cannot intervene. It expands when it is recognized through love and compassion. The transmutation from anything that is not God into God itself is not happening from God itself intervening. It is happening when you recognize that you are God, created from Source. That moment of recognition is what activates the transmutation because you are giving the God in you the permission to be more of itself, and the result is what you call healing. God/Source runs through your blood, cells, and organs, and there is nothing it cannot transmute into its own nature, but only through it being acknowledged.

This is the nature of God/Source.

Let us also look at the creation of these so-called pesticides. They are created by men and women in labs who are focusing on killing what they are calling pests, which are actually organic beings. These labs are not looking at the nature of nature herself. They are intervening from a perspective of war-energy. Their chemists will say, "I will create what will kill the thing that I think is doing harm." Nothing in nature is set up to do harm. It is not the design of Divine.

It is the human ego that is setting up this machine. Humans say that these manipulative ways, en masse, are throwing off the balance of the Earth. Not true, dear ones. It is throwing off the balance of humankind. When humanity experiences and chooses its own Divinity, and surrenders to it, the entire co-creative force of man and planet will flow into an electrifyingly magnificent balance. Humanity is in its balancing act at this time.

Again, we emphasize that Earth, specifically Gaia, will be fine. You have not yet begun to tap into the magic and wizardry that she has to offer. This will happen when and only when you experience the light of God/Source in you and surrender to all its splendor. And we wish to emphasize that you are not surrendering to something outside of yourself—you are surrendering to you . . . yes, you.

M: Then, explain the process of extinction.

AR: Extinction is a choice a species makes for various purposes. Remember that no part of Gaia is ever a victim. It is not possible in Divine. The idea of victimhood is a man-made concept that has emerged from the collective ego. Often, a species that is being manipulated by humans will decide to leave to call attention to the negative effects of human manipulation on your planet. So, it is the choice of the plant, fruit, or animal, or the species within your waters. The more humankind interferes with nature, the more nature will "move away." So, there is no pain or harm that these species are experiencing, but rather a choice and often a part of the collective soul's journey of each species. Gaia is here and exists as a constant mirror of love. She mirrors God/Source one hundred percent of the time. Those species of plants and animals are returning to the planet, and many have come back in newer forms of species that will assist humanity as it rounds its corner into the new Earth.

M: Why doesn't the Divine essence of each manipulated plant and animal stand strong and resist the manipulation?

AR: It has done that in the past. Humanity has been tampering with the power of Divine for thousands of years. When this first occurs, a human will get ill and quite often survive because, as we mentioned earlier, the Divine essence of the human knows what to do, and it will eventually create balance again, because that is what its essence is. When repeated man-made manipulation occurs, over and over, all derived from the ego, the Divine essence of the body makes the decision to move on, to seek the mirror of its own essence, so to speak.

M: That seems as if the Divine is abandoning the human.

AR: Not possible. You see, there is no intervention from Divine. You all often use the term Divine intervention. That is not possible. Remember that the Divine is the All-That-Isness of everything. God does not intervene. That would be assertion and would defy the law of choice and free will. When a human is ill and prays to God to make the illness go away, and in fact that illness does disappear, this is not because God intervened. It is because the human, through the specific prayer, is speaking to and summoning the Divine essence within. Each one of your cells, your organs, your atoms in your body contains God/Source. When you summon that God/Source from within, it rises up like a collective army of love and will take care of all that is not of God that is in and within your body. So, you see, you are your own healer!

M: So, why do plants and animals not do the same thing?

AR: Because the role of the plants and animals is part of the role of Gaia. Gaia is here to help maintain Divine balance in everything. The agreement that all living things within Gaia have made is to participate in that balance. The living things on and under Gaia are choosing to teach humankind true balance. Those souls of certain living organisms that are being manipulated into what you call extinction have chosen to take part in that aspect of the re-rebalancing act. Remember that transitioning is not a terrible thing. It is a glorious path to reincarnation and more. When a species decides to transition or, as you say, becomes extinct, it is merely moving away and on to its next soul-role. The act of its own choice of extinction is its way of showing humankind that what it is doing is out of balance with the true essence of everything. Notice how this has been happening? Books, articles, and organizations are created that shine a light on what humanity is doing to the planet. This was the soul-intention of every species that left. There will always be plants, vegetables, animals, and organisms available for humanity. But remember that if humanity continues to try to upset this soul-balance, humanity itself may morph into something different—not because the plants, animals, vegetables, and organisms will become depleted, but because humankind may itself become exhausted and depleted from feeding into the energy of the ego. Please know that it is not that Divine will become depleted, but rather that Divine will continue to seek its own expansion. It sounds like a kind of abandonment, but that is never true. The essence of Divine is its own existence, and its goal is continual expansion through love. It mirrors only love, and love mirrors it. When humanity chooses non-Divine, Divine moves on to find itself in everything. And the Divine essence that is in every human remains there, but is in a state of stillness, as it cannot intervene. This is why it is so important for humans to navigate their way back to remembering their Divinity. Once this happens, the Divine essence ignites again. Some refer to this as an awakening. It is more of a re-awakening.

This chapter invites us to see cleansing in a radically different light, not only as a way to detoxify the body, but also as a process of realigning with the Divine essence within us. Toxins are not just physical substances but energetic imprints left behind by disconnection and by humanity's repeated attempts to override the natural order. Yet even in the most altered plant, the Divine still lives. And within each of us, the capacity to recognize that Divine essence has the power to transmute distortion into light, both in ourselves and in what we consume.

Awareness is key. The more we remember who we are—expressions of Source—the more we become conscious participants in healing. Gaia, in her wisdom, is not harmed by our manipulations; rather, she reflects our imbalance back to us so we can choose differently. Illness, extinction, and toxicity are soul-level choices and messengers. When we release the illusion of victimhood and remember that the Divine cannot be diminished, we reclaim our role as co-creators of a balanced and love-filled Earth.

Healing does not come from outside intervention. It happens when we recognize the God within and give it permission to do what it was designed to do: restore harmony, illuminate truth, and show us who we truly are.

DISCOMFORT AS
A MESSENGER OF DESIRE

I MUST SAY, it often appears as if the Akashic Records are influencing me in certain ways, such as waking me in the middle of the night. But it's important to know that I accepted my role of bringing the essence and wisdom of the Akashic Realm to the masses. It reminds me of that saying, "Be careful what you ask for." I love this!

Discomfort is often viewed as something to resist or fix. But in this exchange, the Akashic Records revealed something radically different: Discomfort is a call from the soul—a nudge toward desire and alignment.

M: I woke at 2:22 a.m. What's the meaning of this?

AR: This is our time, Mary. We will be having more of these exchanges as long as you respond to our calling in this way. It is much easier for downloads of information to come in through you at these times.

M: I am finding it challenging to be fully awake at these times. What can I do to help myself wake and write?

AR: You are doing it. Be patient. There are no expectations. This is your agreement you made with us some time ago. The more you line up with these interactions, the happier you will be.

M: I want to be healthily skinny and in shape.

AR: Keep thinking skinny, Mary. You had a pocket of passion around this issue yesterday, yes?

M: Yes, at the Inn. This was a similar feeling to one I had many years ago, right before I stopped smoking. I was at a square dance at the home of one of the actors with whom I worked. I remember others much older than me dancing nonstop, and I could not keep up with them. I was out of breath. I wanted to have their stamina.

AR: What works for humans is to think passionately about the change. This is the key to manifestation. Manifestations occur when passion powers them. What trips humans up is when the passions become buried beneath sadness, dejectedness, and/or unworthiness.

You are worthy of everything you are passionate about. Try to think differently about your weight desires. In moments of discomfort, allow the discomfort to power itself into desire. Discomfort actually is desire—the desire of your spirit for something to happen. Discomfort makes you aware that there is something you want.

M: I see that now. So, discomfort is not showing us that something is wrong but rather revealing a desire.

AR: Yes. You can begin to use this tool actively, instead of having it use you. When people feel discomfort, they often allow the energy of discomfort to take hold. When this happens, the thing that is not wanted runs the show. So, when the feeling of discomfort arrives, observe it for only a second. Once discomfort is recognized it disappears, which creates a space for your desire to take hold. This is law. When there is no discomfort anymore, there is only action toward what you want. This is like magic, really.

M: I get this. Earlier, when I got up, I took a moment to tap into how I felt. As soon as I was aware of some discomfort at being up so early (or late), it left me. And I came up with the solution of writing in bed, where I am now.

AR: Yes, this is good to share. We want you all to recognize the difference between feeling discomfort and being aware of discomfort. The feeling of discomfort happens first, then your mind gives it meaning and life. When you feel discomfort in that moment, have an awareness of it first—by awareness, we mean stepping back from it in a moment and observing the idea of discomfort. This will allow space for the energy of desire to emerge to prevent the discomfort from taking hold, and then ideas of actions to attain that desire will arise. When that happens, poof! The discomfort disappears. Discomfort cannot survive in the energy of desire. Desire is part of the All-That-Isness of everything.

Discomfort does not mean we are broken or off track. It means something beautiful is asking to emerge. Once we recognize discomfort as a messenger of desire, it can no longer control us. It dissolves, making space for the next right step. As I continue to honor these Akashic awakenings, no matter the hour, I'm learning that awareness itself is a bridge. It lifts us out of reaction and into remembering. And from that place, life begins to respond in kind.

SOOTHING THE SOUL, NOT THE EGO

OFTEN WHEN WE feel emotional overwhelm or uncertainty, we reach for ways to soothe ourselves, sometimes unconsciously. I have personally experienced this desire for relief. But what if some of the ways we seek comfort are leading us further away from the peace we truly long for? In this Akashic exchange, I wanted to explore the truth behind this craving for lightness and how the ego can cleverly disguise dense choices as moments of freedom. What came through offered a compassionate reminder that our light is always available. We only need to remember how to reach for it with awareness.

M: Lately, I have found myself reaching for things I think will bring relief, comfort, joy, even a break from stress, but afterward, I often feel more depleted, not better. Why is that happening? And how can I soothe myself in a way that nourishes my spirit instead of draining it?

AR: Some choices bring you up, and you interpret that as the way out of crisis energy. That part of the process is good—the part where you know that you want to be lighter, more joyful. What happens is that the ego sometimes tricks you into certain choices.

You see, the ego does not want you to be light and free, for you will no longer need it. So, it tricks you into choosing methods of light and free that begin as just that, yet they are really based in density. Think about how it feels after a night of heavy partying. Going into the party feels fantastic, yes? Then, during the party, you also experience what seems like joy and lightness of being. Now look at how it feels the next morning after heavy partying—sometimes a hangover, lack of sleep, wishing the party were not over. So, the desire for lightness and freedom turned into a dense sense of anything but light and free. The ego loves this. It exists to keep you dense so you will need it. When you are in that dense state, the ego steps in to occupy you with thoughts of "Why did I drink so much? What's wrong with me? I'm sick and now I have to spend the day healing. I don't remember what I said last night."

Now go back to before the party. Remember the feelings of desire for lightness and joy? These are wonderful to feel. They are of the light. Try using that exact same energy and ask that energy to show you how to make it bigger and lighter. It will show you different choices. Maybe you go to that same party, grab a soda or water, and stay and converse from that perspective. Or perhaps you have one alcoholic drink. So, we are not saying to avoid the party. We are saying to go there after recognizing the light that wants you to go there to begin with. When you are feeling stressed or like you need a break, your need or desire for less dense (the stress) can get grabbed up by the ego. This can be tricky. You are absolutely justified in wanting the break (the party). The ego takes you there and encourages low-self-worth activities, disguised as lightening up. When you are aware of this, you can powerfully move this energy in a different direction. It will feel fun, we assure you. The same goes for other dense choices humans make, such as not eating well, or not sleeping, or overindulging in work. The ego loves these activities because they place you into a space of extreme spiritual and physical imbalance. Then the ego can have its way with you. Ego exists in an unreal space of density.

We say unreal because the ego is not what is real. Divine light is all that is real. When you focus away from Divine light, there is this space—a space of non-Divine where ego can take root.

M: Please clarify the role of nothingness and its connection, if any, to the ego. Is it true that in the space of nothingness exists everything?

AR: Yes. It is a powerful space that has been misperceived.

M: You have conveyed that the ego takes hold from a space, a void of some sort. Is it this same space of nothingness?

AR: Let us clarify. Yes, nothingness is actually everything and where truth, love, and all possibilities and choices reside. Everything that you could want is available in this field of possibilities. This quantum space of nothing and everything all at once mirrors the Universe and everything and anything that you could ever imagine. When an individual knows he is Divine, the ego cannot appear. It cannot reside in the space of Divine love. But if that same individual enters that space of nothingness with low self-worth or qualities of un-love and non-Divine, the ego can slip in and the chosen possibilities will manifest as un-love.

M: But I thought this space of nothingness is only of the Divine.

AR: It is simply the energy of nothing—a holder of all possibilities. It does not dictate or judge whether the possibilities are good or bad. It merely matches up with the energy that enters its space.

M: This makes sense to me.

AR: As you move through your life experiencing the third dimension and being a human being, remember that you are

Divine spirit—all of you. The human aspect is like a costume. Know that there are no boundaries—ever. Boundaries are perceptions of the manufactured ego. The ego forms itself from non-Divine. Then it gives itself non-Divine or un-Divine energy, gathers this energy into more of itself, and floats about looking for humans who are in a state of non-Divine themselves. Those moments of non-Divine may crop up from various sources: past lives, past lineage, or subconscious patterns formed during childhood.

So, back to needing a break and choosing to go to the party. The next time this happens, sense the energy of the need first, rest assured that it is justified, and play with it by letting it take you to situations where you become lighter and more joyful. When you do this, you will make choices that expand you increasingly in light. It is that lightness of being— the one that has been spoken of—that will not let you choose dense actions. This is because all that the light desires is expansion and for you to experience the magnificence of who you are: a mirror and steward of God/Source.

I loved learning about the concept that nothingness is where everything exists. How powerful! And that in this space, all possibilities exist! This exchange also reminded me that our desire to feel better is never wrong. It's the ego's subtle hijacking of that desire that can take us off course. The ego thrives on density, confusion, and guilt. But when we become aware of this pattern, we can redirect our choices back toward the light. We do not have to reject the party, the break, or the desire for pleasure. We simply meet it with consciousness and ask, "Will this expand my light?" When we choose from that space, soothing becomes a natural thing. And we remember, once again, that our true nature is not stress, or confusion, or ego. It is the light of the Divine, always ready to lift us higher.

TOO MUCH YET NEVER ENOUGH

HERE HAVE BEEN times when I thought my entertainment career was "over." I had reached a place in my life where I'd won awards, and my creative expressions had manifested numerous successes. Yet I always felt as if it wasn't enough. I wanted more, but the more didn't seem to be coming. As a result, I accepted the idea that this was it for me—that my career was over. As I began to have those thoughts, the creative opportunities also began to dwindle. I now know that I carried a subconscious belief from childhood that too much is not good, that mediocrity is normal, and that wanting more is not possible and can ultimately lead to unhappiness, or worse. I remember my mother sometimes saying, "It's never enough for you, Mary, is it?" Many of you may resonate with this—an authority figure who said, "That's enough. Stop it." Or, "Shut up!" So, the term "enough" became a kind of boundary or judgment, implying that whatever joyful action you were engaged in was "too much." I love what the Akashic Records say here about these words and their perceived and often misunderstood meanings.

M: Why do I always feel as if what I have attained is not enough? Even after success, I still feel this quiet pressure, like there should be more, but I am not sure what that even means.

AR: The words "too much" imply a perception that having too much is not good. We wish for you all to fall in love with "too much." When the ego gets hold of "too much," it turns it into negative thoughts and actions that can potentially harm you or others. You have evidence of this on your planet at this time. Many refer to this time as chaotic. However, too much, when expressed from love and compassion, is beyond amazing. When you honor the beauty of life around you—nature, the animals, the sun, the moon, the planets, the sunrises and sunsets, the oceans and their creatures—and you refer to them as part of the circle of life, often referring to it as magic, you are experiencing the too-muchness of the Divine! "Too much" is part of the Divine design for humanity and the planet.

The perception that too much can be harmful is a human-created trap. There is never too much. There is only more and more and more and more—it keeps going. Expansion has no limit, no end. The saying in your entertainment field, "you are only as good as your last show," as harsh as it sounds, is true, because there is always room for more. Often, you hear creatives, such as authors and artists, say that after their last great painting or novel, they now have a block because they feel as if there is no more from where that came. They manifest a pressure within themselves, believing that their latest work of artistry could never be topped. Another trap. The ego, again waiting in the wings after a profound completed work of some kind, is waiting to insert the thought that "this was it! You are now done! There is nothing more that can be that great!" Oh, dear humanity, this is so far from the truth! Your perceived blocks are merely profound moments of clear, crystal light—poised for the next great Divine download that emerges from the meeting up of your higher selves with the essence of life itself! It is a rich period of time (your time, of course!), a time to wait, watch, and listen. Bask in it when this happens!

We would like to offer a new title here: Too Much and Even More! You see, "never enough" implies lack, and there is no such thing as lack. Humanity perceives those moments in time, when there seems to be nothing happening, as lack, or a missing of something, or a loss. Not possible. There is only more!

The words *too much* and *not enough* are illusions born of limitation. The Akashic Realm reminds us that expansion is the natural state of the soul—there is no ceiling. The ego may whisper that we have peaked, that it's all downhill from here, but the Divine never says such things. The Divine is always saying, *"There is more. There is always more."* And when we meet our blocks with presence rather than panic, they reveal themselves as portals into the next beautiful becoming. So yes, I will keep listening. And yes, I will welcome more.

THE ROLE OF PAST LIFETIMES

BEFORE THIS SESSION, I had been sitting with an unexplainable heaviness—an emotional discomfort that didn't seem to belong to me in this lifetime. I took my concern into my Akashic Records with a simple but honest question: "What am I still carrying, and why does it feel so familiar?" What I uncovered was unexpected. The truths that came forward were not easy to hear, but they gave shape to something I had long sensed but could not name. This exchange helped me begin to connect some of the deeper threads between my past and present.

M: What are some of the wounds from my past that I am here to heal?

AR: Your Records are showing the word scorn. Look it up and feel and sense what comes up for you when you read the definition. You have been carrying this around for many lifetimes. Once you clear this from your body, mind, and spirit, you will begin to experience pure joy—Divine joy.

M: Wow. I can feel something already. Was I scorned?

AR: Both. You were, and you scorned others. But the heaviest burden you carry is the scorn you bore in past lifetimes.

M: Did I do terrible things?

AR: Look up this word, now.

M: Oh, wow. When I looked it up, one of the examples using the word *scorn* was "Poured scorn on my attempts at writing!" Is past scorn blocking my writing?

AR: Yes—writing, directing, living—living in joy.

M: I am feeling so sad right now. Why?

AR: Because you are feeling the feelings of having been scorned so long ago. You came in with this in this lifetime. Part of your role in this lifetime is to forgive your soul for what you have done so long ago. This lifetime has given you such love because it can assist you in letting this past scorn go. You have the love from your mother, Christine, your brother Ronald, wonderful relationships, the amazing animals you have had in your life, and all the people who simply love being with you. You have not understood this truly because you are still wearing the sign of scorn.

M: Will it help me to know what I did that warranted scorn?

AR: Yes and no. We do not want you to go there to remember because you will feel guilty, and it will propel you in the wrong direction.

M: Is this why I would laugh at the expense of others when I was little, and sometimes now?

AR: Yes, you are getting it, Mary. Your past lives contain incidents of having ridiculed people to the point of them killing themselves over it. And the people with whom you lived believed this was a source of power over others—to put them down, to torture them into believing they were worthless, and then watch them disintegrate. This is why you are sometimes drawn to stories about people in history who harmed others with their power.

M: Yes, and it confuses me that I am sometimes intrigued by these stories. It doesn't seem like me.

AR: It is because you were once one of them. Your survival was based on getting rid of anyone who challenged you or threatened to take your power away.

Yes, you were barbarian. Look this up in your history, and you will resonate with this truth.

M: Wow. This is difficult to take in. It just does not make sense with how I live in this lifetime.

AR: That is right. You have been slowly transmuting this past karma, lifetime after lifetime. But the energy of scorn is still inside of you. Yes, you were scorned by the masses. They wanted you eliminated, and that is what they did. They did eliminate you. You were hunted down, but before you were killed, you were held up to be ridiculed and hated and scorned by so many.

Remember, Mary, you have had many, many lifetimes. This one we speak of is the heaviest one for you. It holds the deepest wounds that you are clearing. But before they can clear and heal, you must accept your past, acknowledge it, and forgive yourself. Your soul at that time was not in alignment with your body and mind. You were at an extremely low vibration and have been slowly raising your vibration each and every lifetime since then.

M: How long ago was this?

AR: This was nearly prehistoric. This is also why you have been struggling with your eating issues—meat, no meat, etc. You were an animal hunter and killer, and this was how you survived: by eating the flesh from what you killed.

M: Why did my soul choose that lifestyle of killing and disregard for others?

AR: It was part of your chosen path to work through self-loathing to ascension. Those who kill and look down on others as separate from themselves experience self-loathing. They are separate from love. You were separated from your Divine being.

When you came back in the next lifetime, you began a life of disregard again—because it was familiar to you—but then you experienced love, and it shifted you some, but not until you had caused more pain and suffering to others. But you did shift before you died, so you understood the power of love.

In the next lifetime, you searched and searched for love but never found it, because you were searching outside of yourself. You died having never found love. This is a wound from another lifetime that you are still carrying around today. You have love, Mary, but you do not realize it. Your Records show that you will complete this cycle by coming into oneness with the love you carry inside of you.

M: How can I release my attachments to these wounds?

AR: We want to explain an important concept here. You cannot release attachments because these are not attached to you. Non-light cannot influence light in that way. Light is all there is. Your perceived wounds are simply past-life choices turned into events and experiences throughout all your lifetimes. All energies from all lifetimes are powerful assets for you as you progress into each lifetime. And to be clear, these assets are in the form of the energy only of those lifetimes. You are not bringing the actual events, thoughts, and deeds into each lifetime. So, for example, if you were a leader who harmed others in a past life, when you look at that aspect of you through the Divine light that you are, you can mine the light of that lifetime. What does this mean? In the example of you as a leader doing harm to others, you would have had to wield much power to be able to do the things you did. So, you can pull forward, through intention and knowing, the energy of that power (as it is still with you) and allow it to permeate your present lifetime of love. You see how that energy of that past lifetime of negative service can now be applied to the light?

M: Yes. I do see this. So, all lifetimes play a role continuously in our evolution as humans?

AR: Yes. The other way to transmute those older energies into value in your now time is to be of service to others as much as possible. This transforms all wounds into light. You can be of service through your actions and in your thoughts and prayers.

M: I am having a strange feeling about having made up what was just written about my past lives. I am uncomfortable. Was this my ego stepping in?

AR: Say the opening prayer again, Mary, and come back and tell us how you feel.

M: I feel as if my reaction is rooted in the self-loathing that I might have experienced in that lifetime. It is in my stomach, and I feel lonely and sad.

AR: Yes. But it is not real today. See that, Mary. You have chosen to come into this lifetime as a light being of love, caring for others, sometimes so much that you put yourself last. There is an imbalance here. You see? Once you forgive this past, then you can allow the value of your past to appear now, and you will come more into a balance to live in harmony with yourself and others. We emphasize "in balance." You are no longer that scorned person from so long ago. You have had lifetimes to learn about love and its power. This is the last lifetime that you will have to deal with the heaviness and burden of scorn. It has already transmuted into love! No need to release it! It is not yours anymore, not in its original form. It has been cleared through lifetimes in which you gave up your life for others and suffered for ideas that benefited humanity. You are free. When these feelings of unworthiness come up, stop and put on music that soothes you, settle your mind, and think only of those people in your life whom you love tremendously. This will elevate you up and out of any perceptions of these past burdens that no longer exist.

We want you to know that healing past-life wounds does not erase them from your Akashic Records. The Records are an imprint—there for eternity. But what you can learn to do is to transmute those powerful and often traumatizing lifetimes into powerful light.

Remembering difficult past lifetimes can feel overwhelming; it was for me. The emotions that surface—shame, grief, even disbelief—can make us want to push those memories away. But when we discover these truths from within our own Akashic Records, there's this feeling of being held by the love of the Divine itself. The Divine entourage gently walks with us as we move from remembering into the light and love that we truly are. And from this perspective, we can allow what we remember to emerge and transform into assets that fit beautifully into our present life journey. For me, once I experienced this remembering, it became easy to allow my light to shape who I am now and how I continue to evolve.

SUBCONSCIOUS PATTERNS

SUBCONSCIOUS PATTERNS were not something I thought much about—until I kept running into the same personal blocks over and over again. No matter how much work I did on myself, certain dynamics, especially around power and value, kept showing up in my life. It wasn't until I began working in my Akashic Records that I saw how deeply these patterns were wired in me—not just from this lifetime but from many.

This chapter reveals one of the most eye-opening conversations I've had in the Records around subconscious programming—how it begins, how it lives in us, and how we can begin to see it not as a flaw but as a powerful energetic thread that's trying to show us something essential about our path.

M: What are subconscious patterns, and how can they help us expand into our chosen journeys?

AR: Subconscious patterns are, as many of your quantum leaders are tapping into, patterns that develop when you are young, during your present lifetime. The subconscious begins as a blank slate, not yet developed. This occurs roughly between zero and age seven; however, it can be a wider window of time than that, depending on the individual. During that time, the subconscious, which is still a blank slate, begins to record everything that exists in the world around you as a child: belief systems, perceptions and thoughts about you, how love is expressed (or not)—everything. It is important to know that the subconscious does not judge. It does not know right or wrong, because there truly is no right or wrong. It simply records everything occurring in and around you. Once the subconscious is formed and you begin to mature and grow, the subconscious takes on a role where it runs your behavior from the background of your mind. The conscious mind is not aware of this. Your science has been discovering this truth, and the knowledge about the subconscious that is being brought forward into your mainstream is powerful and absolutely true, we assure you.

People often question why they have habits that do not make sense to them. They are not able to connect them to anything, or they do not seem to understand where they came from. That is because their subconscious is creating these behaviors automatically (from the background), and the conscious is not aware of it and therefore does not understand. As adults, you are all listening to your conscious minds, seeking understanding from that part of yourself, but you will not get it because it is the subconscious that is running the majority of your life.

M: I have experienced this in my own life. I had ongoing what I call "petty tyrants" showing up as bosses throughout my career, and I could not understand why.

AR: Yes, Mary. This was a subconscious pattern that was recorded when you were little—a pattern of bullying that you experienced from one of your brothers and from your father. Your subconscious learned that being treated in that way was normal. You see, the subconscious is a non-judger. It cannot distinguish between positive and negative. It simply records. So, in a sense, it is learning that everything it is recording is part of your world. So, in your case, as you grew up, your subconscious, now running your behavior from the background, tried to find and validate those exact things it recorded because it assumed they were a normal part of your life.

M: So, I manifested the bullying in the form of petty tyrant bosses who were mean to me?

AR: Exactly. When one of these so-called petty tyrants was being unkind to you, were others in your workplace in agreement? In other words, did other colleagues support what your bosses were saying or doing to you?

M: Never. That is what was so confusing to me. I simply could not understand why this was continually happening to me. It went on for some time. Could I have changed this if I had known it was a subconscious pattern?

AR: Absolutely. Let us look at your specific pattern. The first thing is to realize there is a pattern and that it is a subconscious pattern. Some people struggle with the idea that there may be a part of themselves that is running the show without their being aware of it. This is the ego trying to usurp the truth. When you can allow and acknowledge the subconscious pattern, then you are free to work with it. Yes, work with it. You do not want to get rid of it because it is a part of the whole you. It is important to understand, too, that these patterns are not yours, as your Dr. Bruce Lipton teaches. He is correct. They were never yours to begin with. That should alleviate any deep connection to it. Once you have an awareness of it and how it came about—how it got recorded—then your conscious mind can look at it in a new way, as something separate from you. So, in your case, Mary, you can see the bullying as separate from you. Then you can look at how it began, as if you are looking at another child. This way, you are learning about the pattern itself. Next, look at what role that pattern may have in the bigger picture of you, what your chosen path is. Every subconscious pattern plays a role in your soul's chosen journey. Let us look at yours now.

M: In looking at my pattern of being bullied and attracting those kinds of people around me, I learned that I do not have value.

AR: Let us look at the energy of bullying (being bullied). What does it look and feel like?

M: Disempowerment. Being shut down.

AR: And what is the energy of disempowerment? Is it weak? Is it strong?

M: Very strong. Powerful.

AR: Yes. Now, if we can look only at the energy of the bullying, not the events of the bullying, it can become an asset for you today in your life. This is what we mean by mining the energy of something. Please know that we, as your Masters, Teachers, and Loved Ones, are never invalidating your challenging experiences at the times when these patterns were being formed. But what we are wanting you all to see is that the light of the Divine is more powerful than anything. You all are light, no matter what circumstances you have been in. All circumstances come from and lead back to the light. They are tools that feed into your soul's chosen journey. Once you can see these patterns as not owning you, you can separate from them, then look at them like a Rubik's Cube and glean the energy from them. They can then become valuable assets in your lives. The energy of what you have labeled as good or bad is the same energy! It is all energy, and it is all the same. This truth can be quite freeing for you all.

M: Can you give examples of subconscious patterns that may have been interpreted as negative but wound up becoming an asset in someone's life?

AR: Yes. A person who was shut down when they were little. Maybe they were not allowed to have a voice, or they were told they were too big, too loud, or too much. There is an energy around being shut down that is powerful. It takes power to shut someone down, so the subconscious will record that energy as well as the experience of being shut down. When that person matures and is able to recognize this as a pattern in his/her life, and define the energy of it, it can become a tool. That person may become a master speaker because they are willing to mine that energy and channel it into what they are passionate about, in line with their soul's chosen path. They may become activists, speaking on behalf of those who have been silenced. That person will not only know this energy, but they will be a master of recognizing when that energy is appearing in and around them. They will develop a kind of radar for detecting it. These same individuals might excel in acting, or they may become successful lawyers. You see how the energy of the patterns, when channeled through the light of your Divine chosen paths, becomes a magnificent tool?

What I have come to realize is that subconscious patterns are not roadblocks that stand in the way of our growth. They are part of our soul map. When I look at my subconscious patterns through the lens of my Records, I can see that the energy within even the most demanding patterns is a resource for my soul's evolution. The patterns hold power, if I'm willing to step back, see them clearly, and work with their energy. That shift in perspective changes everything. It's what makes the Akashic Records so unique.

ON RELATIONSHIPS

I'VE SPENT MUCH of my life trying to understand relationships—what makes them thrive and what causes them
to unravel. When I brought these questions into the Akashic
Records, I expected to receive insights about compatibility, communication, and maybe even karma. But what came through reframed
everything. The Records spoke about relationships as energetic
co-creations that move within a greater field. It helped me see that
the discomfort we feel in relationships is not always about incom-
patibility. It is often about standing still while the field continues to
evolve. That awareness alone has shifted how I relate to others and,
more importantly, how I relate to myself.

AR: A relationship may not look familiar to you, but aspects
of it will. This confuses couples, because they naturally gravitate to what feels right—and as soon as they unfeel something, they either check out, try to change their partner
(which never works), or try to change themselves (which also
never works).

This is because the field is in continual movement. Even
when you want things to be the same for you in your life,
often there is difficulty—not because you have changed,
but because the field has shifted, and you are unknowingly
standing still.

M: What if the couple is not meant to be together?

AR: They are in some form of relationship already if they have come together for this kind of clarity/healing. Honoring the present partnership while sharing their truths individually will align each one with their own self and their own soul-chosen journey and they will lovingly discover what can be true for themselves moving forward.

The most nurturing relationships, oddly enough, are the ones where the partners know how different they are from each other, while they also continue to live the wholeness that they are. The concept of differences is really about accepted perceptions created to protect oneself from when things appear to change. You search to identify what is happening. That makes you stop and stand still, while the field keeps on moving about. Then, when you do not recognize yourselves because you are no longer in the field, you may get a sense of being lost—looking about and not recognizing the reality around you. Then, your ego (which loves this!) slams in, to convince you that the relationship is not working and never was.

Relationship itself is nonexistent. There is only co-creation as an ongoing journey. When two people realize this, it matters not whether they are in relationship as long as they are co-creating along the energetic movement of the field. This is how human life was designed—as a continuing quantum field shifting and changing and reforming itself differently each and every time. It is like riding a dolphin forever through life!

Passing through each other—not to expand yourself, but upon coming out the other side—you have contributed to the expansion of the whole. This is why, at times, it feels so good riding a dolphin with a partner. The dolphin is the field! It already becomes nurtured and expanded by each human being, and when two or more humans pass through each other in this dance of life, the field is fed with more of its own light, which is what expansion of consciousness truly is!

So, when each individual of a couple becomes fully aware of himself in this way, the ride will be pure joy, Always! Remember, if you stop to question it, stare at it, interpret it, name it, engage it in rituals (to prove it exists to others), all this will do is pause you both, and the field will keep moving on without you. Then, when you look around, things may look different—because they are! Humans interpret this difference in perception and try to figure it all out, blame each other, the relationship, others, or outer circumstances.

Another key thing to remember is that when an individual thinks that they are not feeling deeply in love with the other person—or there is something not quite right about the relationship, such as "it is complete here and there, but not quite there"—the most helpful thing to do is to substitute the word "me" for the relationship, or the other person. One hundred percent of the time, what you are sensing you are lacking is exactly what is inside of you. When we look inside to discover and identify what we want and need, all relationships work!

This reading reminded me that no relationship is ever truly broken. If two people have come together, it means something meaningful is already unfolding. The Records clarified that our discomfort in relationships is often caused by our attempts to hold them in place, despite the fact that everything—energy, growth, intention—is designed to move. Now when I sense distance or friction with someone, I no longer ask myself what's wrong with them or us. Instead, I ask how I may have stepped out of flow with the field. And often, the real work is returning to my center. From there, co-creation becomes possible again—not by fixing or forcing, but by moving with the rhythm of expansion that relationships are meant to inspire.

GOOD VERSUS NOT GOOD

"**G**OOD IS AT the center of everything." This message came to me as I awoke one morning. It felt like a knowing, and it stayed with me, pulling me inward. I opened my Records to explore what it meant and how I might begin to trust the energy of good again—not just in others or the world, but in myself. What followed was a profound exchange about the nature of good, the illusion of false light, and the role of Divine love in returning us to who we truly are.

M: I woke this morning with the words *"good is at the center of everything."* Is this something that we need to be thinking about these days?

AR: Yes, Mary, we want to expand on this idea that appears to be forgotten or buried—cleverly, we add—by the ego. When humans lose touch with their own good—which remains at the center of everything—they begin to fill the space created by this separation with all that is the opposite of good. By being in the energy of separation from one's goodness, one tends to verify that separation by acting as if the good were not good at all. So, the tendency, then, is to create a world that stays away from good—actions and thoughts that have nothing at all to do with the idea or energy of goodness.

But it is important to realize that good never wanes. It is a Divine light force that maintains its power, no matter what.

Thoughts and actions that emerge from the space that is away from good will not last, as they are not of the Divine. They are empty, actually. This is why so many humans are so unhappy today. They have forgotten that they are inherently good.

M: So, how do we find our way back to our inherent good?

AR: Through love. It propels you immediately, like a ricochet, back to God. What happens is that the further away from one's good one gets, the more unsettling it may seem when they are propelled back into that good. This is why it is sometimes temporary, such as for those affected by addictions. They, in your words, bottom out—then are ricocheted back into their goodness centers—then they ricochet back to the distant place away from that center where they had been residing in the addiction. This misperceived space is what they are used to. This is tricky, but once humans realize that good is the root of more good and that this is all there is, they can begin to live freely in their Divine centers, because good is what the center of the Universe is made up of. Living in the "good space" of you will merge you with Divine Source. This is where true happiness lies.

Love was designed as the machine to snap you back to your goodness.

Notice how love has become the reason for all things good. Truly, good is the reason for all things love!

M: Can you define good?

AR: Yes. Good is the base of all things, of all energies, of all beings, of the entire Universe. It is an energetic realm that exists at the center of everything. You will not be able to measure it, for if you could, you would be perceiving it, and perception itself is of the ego. Good can always dodge the ego. It is like a moving target of light. You cannot catch it or grab it or even hold on to it. You can only emerge into its light frequency. When you do, it is as if you are wearing it. Acknowledging its power is one way to be immediately immersed in good. Merely thinking it exists is not enough, for the thinking of it is also a perception . . . ego again. But by acknowledging its power, one automatically "wears" it, and when that happens, all human actions and interactions become based in good.

Happiness emerges when one is in their own good. Peace is also a manifestation of good.

M: Goodness seems to be forgotten on our planet. It also appears to be taken lightly or underestimated.

AR: Yes, indeed it is—for the collective ego of your planet at this time has lured humanity away from its core center of good. Humanity is dancing in this self-created space that it perceives as good. Divine good exists independently of humankind and cannot be manipulated.

M: So, how do we recognize the difference?

AR: When Divine good is present, one will only feel it and know peace, calm, grace, love, and kindness. There will be no other thoughts or actions. When self-created good—or what we can call "ego-good"—is present, it will create a feeling deep inside that something is not right, that something is off. This is why it is so important, especially today on your planet, that humans bring themselves into a space of self-reflection and self-love. When you do that, you get in touch with your Divine intuition, and it is from that space that you will recognize good versus not good. When you have that sense that you are in the presence of not good, or false good, just that realization will ricochet you back to your center of goodness. And from that center, you will make decisions and take actions that mirror the powerful good that lies at the center of the

Universe. When that happens, you, the Universe, and humanity expand all at once.

M: Can you give an example of this?

AR: Yes. You may find yourself at a large gathering where you are introduced to someone you've previously been told has done only wonderful things and has helped others in amazing ways. In fact, it is possible that no one you know who also knows this person has one negative thing to say about them. Now, if you are in touch with your inner Divine, if you know that you are love, and you have experienced the love inside you, and if upon meeting this individual, you sense that something seems off and is entirely different from what others have told you about them—in that immediate instant of having that sense or feeling, you are tapping into your intuition. If you follow that intuition, your next action may be to move away from that person. And what may be happening is that you are seeing the "not good" of that person. He or she may not know this, but you will most likely discover later that there are things about that person or actions they are taking that are not genuinely good at all. This happens frequently. The individual may be out of touch with their inner light, and they may have, in a sense, manufactured actions that portrayed themselves as being of the light. The ego is very tricky. It can con one into actions that appear as light but, in fact, are not.

Another example: there may be a powerful corporation that portrays itself as socially conscious and convinces vast numbers of people that it truly is. It may market itself as producing products and services that help people live better lives. However, someone in touch with their inner light may get an intuitive sense that something is off, and they may decide to dig deeper into that company. They may discover that at the core of its intentions lies the drive to make money, and in doing so, much of what that company offers harms people. This is being revealed more on your planet. Many people can sense that something is not right about these not-good entities or their actions. Because these people are in touch with their own love and light, they can engage with and create ways to bring light to these entities and enlighten others as to the non-truth and non-good of their actions.

M: I am witnessing this quite a bit these days. It seems as if the veils are being lifted from companies and organizations that have convinced the masses they are doing good, only to reveal they are, in fact, causing harm to many.

AR: It is so important that all people get in touch with their inner Divine, that powerful love that is at the core of every human being. When one is in that energy, he or she will always detect what is not good.

M: Thank you for this enlightenment this morning!

AR: We are in love, or maybe we should say "in good" with you, Mary, and with all humanity!

What I received from this exchange is both humbling and empowering: goodness is not something we chase or try to prove; it is the very core of who we are. I've come to understand that when I feel aligned, clear, and peaceful, I'm living from that center of good, and my actions reflect this. When I feel off, or when something doesn't sit right—even if it looks good on the surface—I can now recognize that it may not be aligned with Divine good. The more I stay in touch with my inner light, the more easily I can discern the difference. This Akashic exchange reminded me that the answers to what is true, what is love, and what is good are not outside of me; they are built into the Divine design of my being.

THE FEAR OF WHOLENESS

EVEN AFTER EXPERIENCING moments of profound insight, many of us continue searching—moving from practice to practice, teacher to teacher, always seeking what feels just beyond our reach. This chapter explores why the feeling of wholeness can seem so elusive, even though it is the truth of who we already are. Through the Akashic Records, I was shown that the search itself often stems from a misunderstanding: wholeness is not something we find—it is something we already carry within us.

M: Is wholeness possible on our planet right now? It seems as if we are always seeking this.

AR: Wholeness is not something you can achieve, because you are already whole. Each soul incarnates into a lifetime as a spark of Divine, in all its magnificence. There is no need, ever, to seek to be whole. That is the tricky part of the seeking energy. Seeking implies that you are missing something. You perceive that something is missing. But the thing you are seeking is in you already.

M: Why can't we feel or know that at times? Especially if it is our innate makeup?

AR: Because your ego has tricked you into believing that you are not whole. The ego knows that the more you seek, the more away from wholeness you will become. Perpetual seekers never find the pot of gold at the end of the rainbow. This is why they are perpetual seekers. They gravitate to those who claim to have the magic elixirs for spiritual wholeness, grasp some nuggets of wisdom from them, and then move on. The reason they move on is because they have not discovered what they are looking for. You see, the inner power of your Divine wholeness cannot be found. How can you find something that you already have? Think about the example of someone who has lost their keys—or they think they have lost their keys. They rummage through everything and backtrack their movements like mad to find those keys that they think they have lost—only to discover that they had them in their pocket or purse the whole time. Think of the energy that person has expended, searching for something they never lost to begin with. This is the same with seekers—seekers of God, of truth, of answers to the mysteries of the Universe. There is no mystery to the Universe. A mystery implies that there is something that is occurring, and no one knows why it is happening. Oh, dear ones, the ego loves this mystery dance. It keeps you on a perpetual treadmill, expending energy in the effort to discover what is already there in front of you.

We would like to suggest you exchange the word mystery with awe. Awe is, in fact, when the All-That-Isness of a particular thing, thought, or idea reveals itself—and you, at that exact moment, recognize it as a part of you. You could not recognize it if you were not part of that same thing or idea. Think on this. A fragrant, pungent flower rises before you. You cannot not notice it—especially as it emits its fragrance to draw attention to its beauty. That is part of its Divine design. When you stop to, as you say, "smell the roses," the rose sees itself through you—and you are seeing a part of you as well, all in that one moment in time. This is an example of a moment of "wholeness recognition." That rose will blossom more at the same moment that you blossom. You are receiving a spark of your own Divine wholeness.

It will be helpful to ask your higher power to invite these encounters along the path of your life. So, instead of seeking the answers to something that you think you are missing, watch for those moments when you lose time because something magnificent showed itself to you, or rather, through its existence, showed you to you.

So, why is it challenging to live in your Divine during these times on your planet? You see, the collective ego has formed deep false truths about life itself. It wants humanity to see itself as broken and needing to be fixed. This is the only way that the collective ego can keep itself believing it is relevant. This has created a perpetual, circular flow of focus on need and lack. It has no beginning or end, and it cannot expand. Love expands, also in waves of circular energies. The more love expands, the more the ego uses its own perceived energy to, in a sense, try and dismantle love. But love is like a moving target for the ego because love is always showing itself, reinventing itself, changing its colors, using creative ways to express itself in human beings, and mirroring to them their own light and inner love. The ego cannot recognize this, so it continues to use its same patterns and techniques to lure humans away from love. The ego is not creative. It thinks it is tricky and may be at times. But tricky is not creative. As we may have mentioned earlier in this book, humanity perceives struggle—which is of the ego and not real—only when it has not experienced itself as Divine essence. Think on this. When you feel beautiful, others recognize you as exactly that. And when you experience your beauty, you are experiencing the Divine. And when this happens, do terrible things happen to you? Never. The ego cannot recognize this inner love and appreciation because it is not part of its makeup. If and when you forget that you are already whole and forget how beautiful you are, the ego recognizes itself in you at those moments and takes hold. However, at the exact moment that you come to see your own light, the ego poofs out of existence. Because, as we have exchanged many times before, the ego is not real. Let us explain further. When a person drifts away from knowing their wholeness—their inner beauty—they are then out of touch with the Divine. The space where there is no perception of Divine forms a vacuum, and from that space, a person will begin to take actions that are out of tune with their own Divine—their own beauty, self-love, and self-worth. When this vacuous space sees itself, it becomes the space of the ego. How? When the (healthy) ego of that person who has stepped away from knowing their Divinity looks for what was there (the Divinity) and does not see it, the ego begins to perceive itself. This self-perception of the ego, without love, becomes the ego conscious.

There are examples of this throughout your planet. CEOs and world leaders who begin to act out of integrity are a few examples that are having an effect on Earth right now. They have slipped away from knowing that they are whole and Divine, and they are behaving in ways encouraged by the ego. They have forgotten that they are mirrors of God/Source. We assure you that when they remember who they are, your planet will begin to shift back to Divine, back to love, and back to balance.

So, the most beneficial way that every human on Earth can assist the planet and humanity in its expansion is for each individual to cease seeking and instead look for and swim in the experience of awe. Flow your energy in the direction of beauty and love. And remember that in each moment you experience the profoundness of anything, you are, in that exact moment, being shown how profound you yourself are. This is magnificence to the Nth degree!

This transmission was liberating. The idea that wholeness is not something to strive for but something we already are invites us to stop the endless seeking and instead notice—with awe—what is already present. When we experience beauty, wonder, or truth, it is not just showing itself to us. It is showing *us* to *us!* Our own Divine essence is being revealed.

The egoic mind, on the other hand, wants us to keep searching, keep fixing, keep feeling broken. But the ego can only exist in the absence of our self-recognition. The moment we remember that we are already whole, that we are beautiful, and that we are already connected to the Divine, the ego dissolves—because it never truly existed to begin with.

This exchange helped me understand that remembering our wholeness is not about becoming more spiritual or reaching some final state of enlightenment. It is about choosing, in each moment, to notice what is already shining within us. That is pure joy.

GRAVITY IS A HABIT

T HE WORD "GRAVITY" came to me in meditation one morning—not as a scientific force, but as something energetic, something habitual. I brought it into my Records, curious about what gravity might mean beyond Newton's equations and planetary pull. What unfolded surprised me. The Akashic Records offered a radically different view, one that challenges the way we define freedom, limitation, and our very ability to soar. Could it be that gravity is less a law and more a deeply ingrained belief—a habit of thought we've accepted as truth? I was about to find out.

M: What does gravity mean?

AR: Gravity was discovered by your scientists to explain why you are, in a sense, attached to the Earth. It was perplexing to humans to see a round Earth, know they were on it, and wonder why they were not flying or falling off. Yes, there are many scientific explanations about gravity, and some things about gravity that cannot be explained. One is this from your sources: "Explaining the microscopic behavior of gravity has thrown researchers for a loop."

Then, there is the connection humans make between gravity and weight. These thoughts have been tossed about lots on Earth. Your scientific community believes that gravitational waves exist, but they cannot prove it. However, when you look beyond science, you will unlock powerful tools for your future. Your books are relying on Newton's explanation and equation. He went only so far, though. This baffled him as well.

So, we call it a habit because you have developed a habit of thought around gravity that quite literally keeps you in one place—excuse the pun.

There is a dichotomy between this habitual way of thinking—which literally keeps you in place—and your desires and ideas around freedom. Energetically speaking, freedom is the ability to do anything you wish, without constraints that may stop you. Your habit of gravity is exactly the opposite. Your science shows you that you cannot fly without some assistance or reliance on something to help you fly. So, you think you will not fly without that assistance and so you do not. And because you are in the habit of accepting your laws of gravity, this habit can affect your ability to soar in so many ways. We encourage you to think of the possibilities that will arise when you let go of gravity. When you meditate and experience leaving your body, how do you think that is happening when there is also the acceptance of the concept of gravity? Or, when you have what you refer to as "flying dreams," how do you explain it? You see, you are keeping science and spirituality separate.

Did you ever wonder how you could possibly have those flying and meditation experiences if gravity is a given fact? So, the imagination becomes the explanation. But we are telling you here that your imagination is a direct reflection of—and connection to—the quantum field into which you were birthed. It is who you are. You are not gravity. Gravity is a perception.

M: What is the relevance of this today?

AR: When you change your perception of gravity, you will soar. Gravity is simply a tool of choice for humanity, and a reminder of your ability to stay on your planet for co-creation and expansion. Your belief in it makes it so, not the reality of it. Can you feel the difference? Gravity does not own you. It is not a given, despite what your habitual way of thinking suggests. You get to use it, apply it—or not!

Another interesting thing to think about is how you perceive a tool. Usually, you accept the tool for only what you are told it can do and help you with, yes? However, when you let go of the habit of thought—even around that tool—you can find a myriad of ways to use it! This is so with gravity! Lose your habit of thought around what it is, and it will become an amazing tool for you.

And you may ask, but what can I do with gravity? You will discover this by looking for ways to experience no gravity. When you are free from gravity, you will become immersed in the quantum field, where everything exists. It is there that all the action is taking place—and it is there where your Divine essence resides. Today, you are visiting it in many ways—through deep meditations and communing with nature and animals. Those who slip into a coma or have what you refer to as near-death experiences are flying within this field. This is happening because each individual in these examples is letting go of their perception of gravity, or we can say they have let go of the tool of gravity.

M: So, the soul and the spirit have no gravity.

AR: Exactly, because they do not perceive gravity. Remember that gravity is a human perception derived from a third-dimensional need to explain. When those who have left the Earth plane revisit from time to time, they will often manifest slightly into the third dimension. That is because they are focusing on the concept of gravity to do so, in order for you to recognize them. Or we should say, they are intending gravity—they use it as a tool.

The perception of gravity affects humankind in more ways than science knows. This perception influences your ability to fly and soar in so many ways. You have allowed this tool to make you the tool. You operate so much within gravity's collective explanation that it has weighed you down tremendously as a humanity. The idea that things are only exactly as you see them is a form of your gravity. When you accept that something is a truth that cannot be changed, this is a form of gravity as well. Systems that operate in only one way—and that becomes the only way—are gravity. Religious beliefs that are strict in their dogmas are gravity. Can you see how this earthly perception can be binding and how this can affect your ability to see and experience your own endless possibilities for expansion?

So, are we saying to forget about gravity or resist it? Not at all. It is a tool that is part of your collective soul's choice in this grand incarnation. We are suggesting that you release your habit of thought about its true nature and look at it outside of yourselves. It is not a given, we assure you.

M: The following is a statement about gravity on Google: "The gravitational field is really a curving of space and time. The stronger the gravity, the more spacetime curves, and the slower time itself proceeds. Earth's mass warps space and time so that time actually runs slower the closer you are to Earth's surface."

AR: Let us delve into this idea. It is not the gravitational field that is a curving of space and time. It is not even space and time that are curving. It is the quantum field that is moving and breathing God-essence endlessly, to infinity. It cannot be defined. It simply is. And the idea of Earth warping space and time is also not possible. There is no warping, and there is no time. As humanity experiences its own Divine connection to the Divine itself—in the form of each human being experiencing his, her, or its own Divinity—it is this magnificent choreography that creates the sensations of warping, time change, and shifts. What you are truly experiencing is the expansion of the cosmos through the recognition of God/Source. When God/Source is seen—through humans recognizing God/Source within themselves—the Divine cosmos expands as well, and this, by design, will never end. It is the mystical, magical magnificence of Source itself, and humanity has chosen to participate as a collective soul in this glorious unfolding.

This exchange shifted my understanding of gravity forever. It is not just a physical force—it's also a mental framework, one that holds humanity in place far beyond the physical realm. We have made gravity a symbol of permanence, of things being "the way they are." But when we see it as a tool—one that we can engage with consciously, even release when needed—it becomes a gateway to so much more.

I now understand that gravity is a choice, a perception tied to third-dimensional existence. And when we step outside of it, even for a moment—in dreams, in meditation, in communion with nature—we can remember who we really are: boundless, weightless, limitless beings of light, participating in the Divine expansion of all things. Gravity was never meant to own us. It was meant to serve us. And perhaps, just maybe, it is time we let ourselves fly.

INTERDIMENSIONAL HEALING

THIS READING BEGAN from a deeply personal place. I was struggling with my body image, feeling disappointed in myself, unable to stay on track with health or movement, and weighed down by self-judgment. When I opened my Akashic Records, what came through was unexpected and extraordinary—a powerful invitation into interdimensional healing. My Records revealed that my discomfort was less about weight or discipline and more about a deeper shift—my soul's movement beyond the limits of third-dimensional thinking. What followed was a remembrance of ancient abilities and a blueprint for healing that transcends time, space, and the body itself.

M: I am disappointed in myself these days because I cannot seem to focus or stay on track regarding exercise and health. I feel bad about this.

AR: No, no, do not feel bad. Bad is not you. Bad does not even exist. Take this thought and discard it immediately. Simply move forward in terms of exercise as you feel it. Ask your body to let you know what it needs, whether it is rest, a walk, or a walk and run. Really listen to your body, Mary. It will tell you what it needs, and this will soothe you.

M: I am so uncomfortable in my body.

AR: This is because you are disconnecting from one realm into another. You have left the third-dimensional field of energy, so your body is in shock a bit.

M: So, how do I get my body to feel good being in a different dimension?

AR: Hard to do. You are resisting letting go. If you try to let go of your connection to your body, we promise you: you will not die. You will simply shift into other dimensions. Just know that this is possible. In another lifetime, you knew how to shape-shift effortlessly. One can only do this when one releases the idea of being third-dimensional. Your body will not leave you. It will simply transform itself—cells and all—from one dimension to another, and back and forth, as you choose.

M: What is the benefit of doing this?

AR: When you move between and among dimensions, you receive spontaneous healing energies. This is immensely powerful. You acquire fields of power that you can bring back into your third-dimensional form and use in the now of your time. Reread this often, and you will begin to understand how to do this. Long ago, you were able to function daily by doing this. You would travel interdimensionally and become revived repeatedly, which is why you lived many, many years—into the hundreds and beyond. There is eternal life within dimensions. Mary, begin to think on this, and it will happen for you. Because, as you ponder this, you will remember the process and begin to activate it again. You will find joy that you have never experienced, we promise.

Remember that everything is energy, and energy never dies. So, you have the energy of not only every lifetime but also every interdimensional experience within your DNA.

M: What is the key to making this happen?

AR: Silence . . . thinking on it . . . trusting in it. Knowing you can shift back and forth just by thinking on it. You do not have to meditate. You simply need to believe it and think on it. Wish for it. Know it is a part of you—a process that you were a master of throughout many lifetimes. Trust in it.

M: How will I know when it is happening?

AR: You will not know—not in your mind. But you will begin to look and feel younger, we promise. When you look in the mirror, you will see yourself differently. You see, interdimensional movement is beyond cellular. It is beyond physical. It is knowing—that is all—truly knowing. Be certain that you can travel in this way, and you will.

Every time you access your Akashic Records through this dialogue, you are communing with another dimensional field. You trust that what you are receiving is correct and true, yes? It is just more of that.

M: Can I request that I receive something within these other dimensions?

AR: Absolutely. But you must travel there to receive them.

M: How do I know which dimension to go to?

AR: Begin to research interdimensional travel. Because you are asking, you will be guided to the resources that will assist you. The energy within the higher dimensions is all-encompassing, all-powerful, all-healing, all-good. There are masters on your Earth that are holding the Earth in balance, mainly through interdimensional travel and interdimensional work.

Your archangels reside there, so when you go, you are passing, literally, right through their love energy fields. When you return to your third dimension, you bring that love directly into the Earth plane. And you will rejuvenate in the process. It is amazing, Mary. You will see.

M: Is this my work ahead? Am I to dive into metaphysics, and heal in this way—for me and others?

AR: You are at a crossroads right now in your career. Do not be afraid to enter into newer territories. Remember that the old thought forms and old paradigms are nonexistent. You are still holding on to some of them. Directing, for example. You are looking at that in a third-dimensional way, and it is keeping you stuck. Remember, Mary, that directing is leading. Take this time right now and intend to travel interdimensionally. Do not be afraid of it. What you will bring back to your third-dimensional plane will propel you into becoming the leader your Records show you to be. You are afraid to shift. Do not be afraid. Let go. We promise you: it will bring you joy, love, and solace.

M: So, what is the very first thing I need to do to begin this new journey?

AR: You are approaching this from a third-dimensional perspective, which will prevent you from leaving third dimension. Get it? Stop thinking in third dimension. Just ask, trust, and forget about it. As we have said, research the outer dimensions, and you will find ways to begin this journey. We also encourage you to open your Records as you begin. As a reminder, you are listening right now to another dimension—the dimension of your Akashic Records. You will see that when you come away from this session, you will feel better. You will sleep better this evening. And you will wake up tomorrow with innovative ideas about this topic. Write them down.

M: I understand. I am going to trust. And relax. Thank you for this loving dialogue.

Each time I reread this Akashic exchange, I become more invigorated. What began as a vulnerable moment—feeling frustrated with my body and out of sync with myself—opened into an exhilarating revelation about my Akashic journey. To learn that I already carry within me the ability to travel interdimensionally—to shift beyond the limits of the third dimension and receive healing from realms beyond form—is huge. It triggers a remembering and an invitation to let go, trust, play, and reawaken an ability I once had and still do.

This revelation is not just for me. It is for all of us. Every soul has access to this Divine capacity to move between dimensions—to gather healing, energy, clarity, and peace. We are not bound by the physical limitations we've been taught to accept. We are multidimensional beings, already equipped to travel, heal, and expand. I emerged from this dialogue feeling lighter, energized, and ready to step into this next phase of my evolution—not just as a seeker, but as a traveler, a gatherer of light, and a bridge between worlds. And, so can you.

IMMORTALITY

I HAVE BEEN THINKING about immortality for a long time—not just whether the soul lives on, but whether we, as humans, have the ability to remain in physical form far longer than we've been led to believe. I've always had a feeling that something about the way we understand aging and death does not add up. So, I finally brought this question into the Akashic Records.

M: I've been hesitant to ask this question about the reality of immortality.

AR: And why, Mary?

M: Maybe I'm afraid that it will not be true.

AR: Well, perhaps this is the perfect time to exchange on the idea of immortality. Immortality is humanity's perception that you, as humans, do not end. This, we assure you, is not possible. To clarify, consider this double negative: you do not "not end." You simply transform and go on. There is no such thing as an ending. How and when you transform is your choice, always. There are absolutely no limits to anything.

M: Well, we know that our souls move on, indefinitely. But what about our human bodies? Can they continue to exist?

AR: Yes. This is how much power you all have been given. It is your birthright to choose how long you want to stay and live in your present form as humans.

M: This will stir up many responses from people. In my heart, I've always known this to be true.

AR: Yes, we see this in you. There are examples throughout your Earth's history of individuals who lived into their hundreds. Moses of your Bible, for example, and many others—many more than your history has told you.

M: Was it kept from us? If so, then why?

AR: The ego. Humanity's need to maintain power over itself. Consider the implications and results of your entire humanity accepting that it will end. Believing that you will end at some point encourages ideas and processes not only to make your life easier while you are alive and well, but also to prolong your life—through powerful systems that have given themselves that power—the power to engage in the length of your life. Your systems determine and tell you that you are healthy, sick, vulnerable—and worse, that you will die in predetermined amounts of time. We assure you that the only reason humans appear to "end" at certain ages is that you are all being told this. As this false, perceived reality emanates around your planet, it seeps into your consciousness and can become a belief—and therefore your reality.

M: How can we realign with our birthright to remain on this planet for as long as we wish?

AR: Simply know it to be true—because it is. Many ascended masters in your history have remained in human form far longer than was believed possible at the time. And why did they eventually leave? They chose to transition as part of their souls' journeys. You see, you have a choice about everything in your lives. Every . . . thing!

M: How can we break free from the grip of these belief systems that perpetuate the idea that we are going to die?

AR: You all must step away from these systems, as much as is possible, as we know that life can be challenging when one walks their enlightened path at this time in your history. We encourage you to follow only your intuition. Start to practice this in increments. Once you become familiar with the voice inside you, you will no longer be influenced or attached to the various voices outside of you. We have spoken within these pages about how to reconnect with the Divine power within.

M: But why do humans begin to deteriorate in body and mind as they get older?

AR: Because they believe that to be true! Look at how often humans notice in each other that they do not look their age. Some say it is because of their genes. This is not the reason. The reason is that they are experiencing their own Divine joy— each and every one of them. Another misperception lies in the idea of medical anomalies. There is no such thing as a medical anomaly. In fact, we would prefer that you eliminate that word from your dictionaries. That word "anomaly" evolved from the inability to explain something or some event that does not fall in line with the perceived beliefs of your time. There is nothing that needs explaining, because everything exists for a reason and purpose as a part of Divine choreography. There are no ends and no limits—ever. We invite you all to step into the stream of all possibilities from your hearts and higher selves, which know there are never endings, just continuations according to your right of choice. If you prefer to continue to live indefinitely and healthily in human form, then it will be so. Your cells and organs will align with this knowing, specifically because your cells are expressions of the All-That-Isness of Source itself. They inherently seek wholeness and balance, and they only know immortality.

What came through surprised me, yet it made sense. The Records confirmed that immortality—or at least the choice to remain in human form for as long as we desire—is not only possible but is part of our human design. As the Akashic messages flowed through me, my cells responded with a certain recognition. Immortality is not a fantasy; it is a remembering. Our bodies, like our souls, are expressions of Source. They are not destined to deteriorate—only trained to. The Records remind us that we have inherited more than we've been told. Longevity, vitality—even physical continuity—are all encoded within us.

The truth of immortality lives in the quiet, unwavering knowing that we were never meant to fade away.

THE SIXTH MASS EXTINCTION?

LATELY, THERE HAS been a lot of talk about the possibility that humanity is heading toward a sixth mass extinction. When I first heard this, I felt a wave of both dread and curiosity. Could it be true? And if so, what does it really mean from a spiritual perspective—not just through the lens of science or media headlines? I brought this question into my Akashic Records, seeking insight from the Divine. What I received reframed everything.

M: It has recently been concluded by two of our esteemed and high-conscious teachers, Dr. Bruce Lipton and Gregg Braden, that humanity is currently in the throes of a sixth mass extinction. Is this true?

AR: To a degree, yes—but it is not as literal as you think. Also, remember that Dr. Lipton says, "Crisis ignites evolution." He is correct. Humanity, at the time of this exchange (2021), is in crisis. Everything that man has created from its own perspective and not from its Divinity is collapsing. Anything that is not of the light of God/Source, you see, is not real and cannot last.

M: But how can the damage collapse?

AR: Let us explain further. This is the collective ego trying to run the show. This collective ego is not real—it is non-light that becomes the illusion of good things, the illusion of progress. Notice how your advancements in technology throughout the past hundreds of years are now entrapping you. These per-ceived advancements are veering you away from your inner power. A prime example is the so-called coronavirus and its accompanying slew of vaccines. We say accompanying be-cause the vaccines are in the same energetic category as the virus. Both became manifest from the global manipulation in which men and women are participating. These men and women are operating from their ego consciousness, not from who they truly are! Scientists, doctors, and now massive num-bers of human beings claim that the vaccines are the answer to protection from the virus. But think on this: If the virus and the vaccines have the same energetic components (non-Di-vine), then how—and why—would one protect one from the other? Not possible. And here is a Divine fact that will shed more light on this issue: Every human being who has not con-tracted the (perceived) virus did not because they know who they are. What we mean by this is that they know they are whole. They may not consciously know this, but they innately operate day to day from that knowing place. So, an individual who did not contract the virus may have decided to stay away from crowded situations, gently supported their immune sys-tem with good, natural nutrition, and spent time in nature—not from fear, but from a sense of knowing that all is well. On some level, whether consciously or subconsciously, they know they are co-creating from Source—that they are a part of the whole of humanity, here to do good. When you recognize this inner state, this essence of you, you cannot be in fear. Fear has no place there. It cannot exist when you know, experience, and emanate this light that you are. Fear is part of the ego. It is a married partner to the ego conscious. It can take hold when a human is in a state of not knowing they are Divine es-sence—when they do not allow themselves to experience the beauty of that Divine essence and the wonder and beauty of the planet herself.

The reality is this—all is well, all the time. This is a hard one for you all to grasp, because you are looking through the misperception that everything is crashing down on you. What is crashing down now, in your time, is the collective ego. And when you look at the world around you through the lens of the ego, you become a part of it, often without even recognizing it. When the ego is recognized and given attention, it grows increasingly. It makes itself relevant because, when it is relevant, it has a reason to continue to exist, you see. So, attention to it and on it keeps it (thinking) it is running the show. But we assure you, it is not running the show. How can something that is not real run the show? Not possible.

Not until humanity accepts this Divine law—that all is well all the time—will it then be able to move through and past the ego-driven global crisis. Every time you feel into this truth it will ignite something in you, a power that will create more thoughts and actions that evolve you, as a humanity, to your highest good.

M: And what of the beautiful living animals and organisms that are becoming depleted on Earth? Is this a result of the collective ego?

AR: Exactly true. Yes. Here is how it began. Humans began to enjoy the fruits and goodness that the planet had to offer. They reaped them, exchanged them, and shared them with each other. This was God-given balance. You call it the circle of life. Animals, organisms, plants, and trees participated in this natural dance. They willingly came to the planet to participate with humankind in this endless exchange of Divine energy. Humankind was designed to be a participant in this circle.

Then—as we have shared before—man began to focus more on his own image. The reflection that man saw of himself in the waters was just that—a reflection. It was not a duplication of him, which is how he interpreted it. As this reflected self became more real for him, man then began to feed into his reflection, giving it power and strength. Then came a sort of addiction to his reflected self, and then it transformed into man's self-image—even when he was not looking into the pool of water at his reflection. Next, his self-image began to dictate how he should live, and the ego was born. Ego knows it is not real, but it also knows that it can trick humans into thinking it is real. So, when this began to happen, men—more than women, we might add—began to listen to the messages from their newly discovered self-images. This discovery gave men the idea that they were different and more special than others, and that they deserved anything and everything from a place of individual desire. They took actions that would only benefit their self-images. Others began to also experience their self-reflected images, and they, too, began to take actions that answered the call and dictates of these self-images. Do you see now how your planet has arrived at this pivotal point in your time?

M: Yes. And will this giant ego-conscious state we find ourselves in collapse?

AR: It is already collapsing. And Divine Gaia is helping to dismantle it. When you have massive storms, earthquakes, tornadoes, volcanoes, and floods to the degree that they are happening, this is Gaia showing you that you cannot control survival from a place of ego. Until now, men and women have been working on taming these events, but not through Divine actions. They have been responding to these massive shifts by listening to their ego. They have forgotten that they are Divine beings. For example, companies that have the resources and influence—power that could be channeled through Divine intention—are instead choosing to offer solutions that primarily benefit themselves. They are listening not to their souls but to the ramblings of their self-images.

This is happening across your globe. However, there are those human beings who are connected with and listening to their inner Divine, and they know that the only way through this crisis is to collectively join hands in love and peace and act accordingly. Only through this joining can the planet and humanity collectively circle back to its original Divine state.

What the Records revealed is that the extinction concept is much more than the loss of life. It is about the collapse of systems and beliefs that were never built in the light to begin with. Anything created from the egoic mind is falling away. We are not witnessing the end of humanity but rather the end of illusions, false power, separation, fear, and the distorted self-image that has disconnected us from Source. Yes, species are vanishing. Yes, the planet is shifting. But Gaia is not punishing us; she is rebalancing, with love at her core. Ego—the massive construct of separation and illusion—is losing its grip. Our role now is not to panic, but to remember that all is well. Always! This is Divine law.

THE CORONAVIRUS

OLLECTIVELY, WE HAVE emerged from an event that tested every facet of our humanity: the coronavirus pandemic. It shook the foundations of daily life across the globe and changed how we lived, how we loved, how we related to each other, and how we connected to the Divine. In the thick of that period, I opened my Akashic Records to seek clarity beyond the noise. What I received was not only surprising but also deeply instructive and resonates with relevance even now.

AR: Your world is twirling in fear and resistance right now, and we want to share about what is most important. Because of the global nature of this event, every human on your planet is now listening.

M: What is happening, and why?

AR: There is a form of extinction occurring right now. We know this is a difficult word to hear, but the planet is tipping, in a sense. Greed, birthed from the collective ego, has grown to unbalanced proportions.

M: But massive planetary events have happened before. Was the ego always responsible for them?

AR: There certainly was ego in every time period on planet Earth, but humankind was never operating both individually and globally in such destructive ways as in today's time period. The machines and technology created by humankind have surpassed man's ability to live in choice.

These technologies have slowly been creating a wedge and a separation between humans and the Divine. In past times, there was no technology, so when events occurred, humans still knew who they were: Divine beings sharing the fruits and beauty of planet Earth, of Gaia. They were not able to drill into Gaia's surface out of greed, or torture and massacre millions and millions of animals for profit. What they did do was imprison people for their beliefs and create structured religions that separated people from their Divine. These were the events that surrounded the planet in earlier times. But remember, those events were not global—or we might say, they did not begin globally. Look at your planet today. There has evolved a mantra of "faster, easier, and now."

M: I am seeing a very troubled and dark planet right now. Is this me, or is this what you are showing me?

AR: Mary, we are in co-creation during these exchanges, so it matters not. We cannot promise anything, but we can show what is written in the Akashic Records. And we can show you what is written in your Records.

M: Okay, so do my Records show me surviving this catastrophic event—and is it catastrophic?

AR: We can let you know that you and Christine are in a safe space right now. You may need to move at a later date, depending on the choices made by your collective areas. It is critical to stay connected to Divine right now—through prayer, meditation, laughter, creativity, and imagination—but be careful that your imagination emerges from your connection to Divine and not from the fear that is swirling around your planet right now. We want you all to know that fear is not real. It is simply a focus away from love and the Divine. The challenge right now is that the nature of this global event is imposing separation from each other. So, those who do not know they are Divine beings will be lost, and, in many cases, will transition. Isolation for lightworkers can be an amazing time for expansion. But for those who are subject to fear or greed, they will suffer more from the lack of Divine connection than from the supposed virus.

M: So, you have not referred to the word virus. I felt a reluctance to write that word. Why?

AR: Let us talk about it now. This is another example of humankind interfering with nature. Yes, nature created a form of this virus from an animal. This is true. But then, scientists working within an ego-based system decided to turn it into a killer. And when greed runs amok, you end up with massive numbers of people being affected by it.

All viruses are composed of energetic signatures. If you can measure energy—which you are capable of doing today—you can identify the signature of this particular virus. Once you have its signature, then you can change or manipulate it further to match the signature of a healthy human cell. So, you can completely transmute any deadly virus into nothing more than another healthy cell. And then it can be used for healing. Imagine that! That is why the animal that was first discovered to have this supposed virus passed it on to begin with. There is nothing in nature that is harmful. It becomes harmful when you change its original Divine, energetic signature.

M: Do scientists not know this?

AR: Most of your scientists and biologists are working within ego-driven, greed-based systems, so they acquiesce. And when your biologists and scientists do discover the truth, they are usually fired, disappear, or become what you refer to today as whistleblowers. This area—the identification of specific signatures of disease—is part of quantum physics. Scientists today are still utilizing the ideas of a past science, compartmentalized by an older paradigm. Your planet has expanded, so your actions in response to it must also expand. Your scientist, Royal Rife, knew about this all. He worked with the idea of identifying the frequency of a diseased cell and from there worked to eradicate it without harming other cells—by sending into the body a frequency that was higher than the diseased one. The higher frequency wiped out the diseased cells without harming the good ones. The basis of your health systems in terms of the eradication of disease is focused on the concept of a vaccine as the solution. This theory was birthed from the idea that if you plant a small portion of the disease into a human, they will become immune to it. In some ways, yes, this is possible, but not good. When you ingest a vaccine, you may become immune to that particular disease at that specific time. But the energetic signature of that disease remains in your body. If and when your immune system becomes compromised, that diseased energy will activate itself all over again.

Now, let us discuss an amazing tool you all have right now. As individuals, you each have the power to move and transmute energy. So, you each can transmute the energy of this perceived killer, even before you are near it.

M: But how can we do this without knowing what that energy signature is? And I thought energy is always moving and changing, so how can it have a definitive signature?

AR: You are thinking now like your scientists and basing your question on perceived facts. Anything that shows itself to be out of alignment with God/Source will manifest in a way that is recognizable. This is why you all often focus on the world being bad. It is what is showing up. Lack of God/Source is shadow perceived as fear. So, in a sense, when it shows up, you can see it and are experiencing its signature. Now, stay with us here. Once you experience its signature, you immediately know how to change it. It is human nature. Infusions of love, compassion, kindness, joy, and happiness will eradicate it immediately. Poof!

M: But we don't know what the virus looks like. We can only see that it can potentially kill us. So, how can we identify its energy signature?

AR: You do not want to identify it; you want to sense its nature and send it love and compassion and infuse it with the intention to transmute itself into light. In essence, raise your vibration, think on this virus, and from that raised vibration, pound Divine love into it. It will bust open and become healthy. We understand that there are many on Earth right now who may not understand what we are imparting. However, there are more lightworkers right now who are questioning what this virus is and how to best serve its eradication. We are emphasizing that it is not an eradication. It is a transmutation.

M: How can scientists serve this idea?

AR: Science will not serve the one-on-one transmutation idea. It is not capable of this because it is primarily third-dimensional, fact-and-data-based. However, as more individuals access this power within themselves, there will be less and less need for science. It is already happening on Earth as more people access natural methods for health and wellness and feed less into the often dangerous, ego-based pharmaceutical system. When scientists learn to apply energy measurements in their protocols, there will be less disease and less need for drugs. The solutions lie in quantum physics.

M: What is the difference between vibration and energy?

AR: Energy exists always. Vibration is the measured result of energy. Quantum physics will evolve into a new protocol for working with energy and vibration in your future.

We want to speak about resistance and how this interacts with what is happening on Earth right now. Resistance is the chosen denial of the truth of a moment. It creates an energetic field around it that then becomes a perceived experience. Then the experience is interpreted by people as positive or negative, which is the ego stepping in to identify the energetic field. When individuals are balanced and know their Divine connection to Source and also recognize themselves as Divine, they will not perceive the resistance whatsoever. Therefore, it cannot and will not affect them! See how this can relate to your global event right now? Your planet became terribly unbalanced around the notion of resistance and separation. The design of Divine is continual balance, so Earth and its lightworkers are creating the new balance. Yes, many will transition, but remember that every soul that transitions at this time is stepping into their Divine design—each soul's chosen path. The reactions of doom and gloom are the resistance to the truth—that Earth is needing to rebalance. What does this rebalance mean? It means love, compassion, kindness, giving and receiving, joy, happiness, and honoring the Divine in each and every human. This is the truth of humanity and why Earth was created.

Let us refer back to the energetic signature of this perceived virus. It is not a virus. It is an energetic signature—a combination of the signature of the cell from the animal that first had it with the added components (and their energetic signatures) of the scientist or biologist. It is specifically the energy signature of this virus that is not a match to the cellular signatures of human cells. We want to reiterate that by raising your vibrations through deep meditation, expressions of love and joy, and deep connection to the Divine, you can speak to the energy signature of the virus, whether it is in your body or millions of miles away. And you can transmute it into love.

Because humans are in a state of self- or state-mandated isolation, this is how the virus will end. If you were not isolated and practiced the transmutation method we described, it would transmute it into healthy cells as well.

M: So, when we are, say, meditating, how do we speak with this virus without knowing its energy signature?

AR: The signature is the ongoing and repeating way that the virus is expressed. We are speaking about energy, not linear measuring. Think about how you immediately sense when walking into a room filled with people, who is good, bad, odd, or wacky. Or how you will immediately gravitate to a person. You are not consciously thinking this—it is your energetic signature urging you in a certain direction because your signature is looking for its matches in energy. This is where the idea that "you are or become who you hang out with" comes from—and it is true.

We realize that these concepts may feel airy and non-attainable to some, but we assure you that this is part of the design of the human race. It is quantum. Your scientists will not be able to measure the "virus energy signature" without applying the laws of quantum physics. And when they do, there will never be what you refer to as disease. Thousands of years ago, there were not diseases as you have today. This is because thousands of years ago, humans were extremely connected to Gaia and the Divine. Ancient wisdom, which is now being received again, operates from a knowledge of energy fields and their signatures. The Indigenous had no need to measure them. They simply tapped into their signatures and transmuted and changed them at will. Today, you call it an anomaly or magic. But it is very real.

M: Is spirit intervening?

AR: This is an excellent question. Yes and no. You see, throughout this lifetime, there have grown millions of lightworkers and ascended humans who—through their connection with the Divine—have had an amazing influence on your planet through their invocations of spirit and nonphysical Divine beings. The Holy Spirit and its entourage of angels, archangels, nonphysical masters, and so many more groups that serve the Divine are interacting with humans continuously. Massive numbers of humans invoking spirit means massive spiritual intervention. But our intervention is more of a co-creation with humankind, according to the design of the Divine or Source. Spirit can nudge humans toward their Divine design, but ultimately, humans have free will and choice. This is where you find yourself at this time. The world is tipping right now, and if you watch carefully, you will observe the specific systems that are breaking down. One is the financial system. It was designed to entrap humans under the rule of those who created it and who oversee and manage it today. But remember, money is not real. That is why it may be one of the first systems to fall. It was never real to begin with. It was created out of ego-conscious energy. And since the ego that we often speak about is not real, then the monetary system also is not real. Love is real, and when love rules, anything birthed or existing from the ego simply cannot exist.

Now we would also like to speak about nature. Your planet rules by nature. There is nothing that can surpass the power of Gaia. Nothing. She is Divinity in its purest form. Therefore, any time individuals or large numbers of people return to nature, they are always purified. When you interact with any aspect of Mother Nature, your cells engage in a joyful dance. This dance is like a puppy when it runs to its mother. Each human cell is structured exactly as nature. This is why people are drawn to vacation in nature. Their cells are urging them to bring them home! We encourage your entire planet to return to nature as much as possible.

We want to add more about the supposed virus that began in an animal. The "virus" was not harming the animal. It was simply a cell that lost its way energetically. It integrated itself into the overall energetic signature of that animal. The animal would have naturally gravitated to a part of Gaia, whether through the ingestion of a specific plant or other animal, and it would have innately transmuted that lost cell into wholeness again. But what happened was that a human intervened, extracted the lost cells (we cannot refer to it as a virus because it is not), and manipulated those cells into something that would be used in warfare. The energy and mission of this mutation became so powerful that it was only a matter of time before it would need to manifest its destiny, which is to harm. This is the potential danger that exists in your laboratories, where cells have been manipulated into that which is far from their natural state of being.

M: Since the lost (weaponized) cells have a specific energetic signature—and are perhaps searching for a match to that signature—we cannot attract those cells if we are not an energetic match, and therefore cannot catch the virus. Is this true?

AR: Yes. This is true. This is why some people died during this time, and others were not touched or affected by the "lost cells" (perceived virus).

M: I am resonating with this greatly.

AR: Yes. And there will be more to impart as Earth shifts and changes, but remember, the natural, innate state of the planet is balance. Stay in love with each other at this time. It is critical for balance to be reached once again.

This exchange was surprising and new to me, yet somehow affirming too. The Akashic Records did not refer to what was happening as a virus; they called it a cluster of lost cells carrying an energetic signature—one that was manipulated and weaponized. They explained that illness is not random; it is energetic. When we maintain a high vibration—through love, joy, nature, and Divine connection—we are never a match to the frequency of discordant energies. And if there is no match, there is no attraction, and therefore, no disease. That understanding changes everything we have believed about disease.

I felt something different during this exchange—an energetic pause, a withholding, perhaps concern. It was as though my Masters, Teachers, and Loved Ones were choosing their words with great care, threading their responses through the lenses of both free will and Divine timing. It reminded me that they cannot override our free will, but they can reflect truth in a way that helps us remember why we are here. And maybe that's what this time has been about—a global opportunity to reclaim balance and return to love.

THE MIDDLE EAST SITUATION

EFORE SPEAKING AT Unity Church in Santa Barbara, I felt a strong inner nudge to open the Akashic Records of the Middle East. What came through surprised me—not the intensity of the message, but its profound simplicity. The situation, so complex on its surface, was revealed to be an amplified projection of humanity's collective ego consciousness. The guidance I received offered a radically different approach—one rooted not in resistance, but in warrior love. The following is the exchange, which I shared during my talk at Unity.

AR: That situation is in desperate need of leaders—leaders in the form of light warriors.

Let us exchange about what this looks like. This is a time in your history when each one of you, including those engaged in the firing of weapons, needs to step up to the plate and look directly into the eye of the collective ego. It is this collective ego that has grown into this dimension of war. We call it a dimension because it—this collective energy—is not real. Love is real. We realize this may sound trite, but never underestimate the power of love, especially when it takes on the form of warrior love.

What does warrior love look like in action? It begins with a gathering of individuals around this situation, who band together to create systems and solutions that are only of love, kindness, and unity. We will give examples of this, and it will rely heavily (to begin with) on your imaginative powers.

There are soldiers right now in that area who are dealing with what it feels like to kill. Humans call it PTSD, and when they return from the war, they try to eliminate it or dissipate it. We are not minimizing the horrific effects on men and women in these situations. But when you all begin to gather into groups outside of this war and outside of this major area of conflict and use your imaginations to counter the divisiveness, the energetic field of the collective ego that has grown for so many years in that area will begin to dissolve.

Search and find those soldiers who, in the moment of pointing their guns to shoot at children or other vulnerable people, did not do it. Dear ones, they exist. Every human being on your planet is not designed to hate and kill. That is the work of the ego, which ramps itself up as it fears its own demise.

When acts of kindness infiltrate those arenas of war, those acts emit a Divine energy that punches a hole in that collective ego and eventually dismantles it.

Use your imagination to spread innovative ideas, new stories, and to create new models of love and acceptance. It can only happen when you begin to do this in groups of twelve or more. Create movements, not marches. Do not scream no at one side or the other. That is what this collective ego desires—it desires division. Turn off your news. Create news platforms that only focus on the light of the situation—the love that this situation is currently showing you. You may say that it is not there, but we assure you, there is light in those areas. You are now in the middle of this hotbed of confusion. Step around it, as Jesus did, and as Gandhi did. They endured hurt and pain, and they continued to walk in the name of love—for each other and for your planet and everything that lives and breathes on it.

This is the time to pick up your golden swords or lightsabers and slice through this ego-manufactured energy field with loving, kind, and compassionate action.

Of course, the Akashic Records did not offer policy or political solutions. They offered something far more powerful: a call to rise in Divine action. This Divine message reminds us that the Middle East, or any region steeped in violence, is not merely a place of crisis but a portal for awakening. When enough of us begin to hold the vision of healing, compassion, and unity—when we gather not to protest but to imagine and embody peace—we punch holes in the egoic energy that perpetuates division. Warrior love is not passive. It is the fiercest force on Earth. And now is the time for each of us to wield it.

IS THE END OF EARTH NEAR?

AT THE TIME of this exchange, and to this day, I have been reading and hearing more about potential planetary endings, theories of supernova events, and fear-based scenarios that seem to be gaining traction in both the spiritual and scientific communities. With so much uncertainty in the air, I opened the Akashic Records and asked directly: "Is the end of Earth truly near?" The following is what came through:

AR: There is no such thing as an end. Everything continues, possibly in different forms, but everything lives on.

There is this unending (pun here) need for humanity to frame everything. By this, we mean placing boundaries—of thoughts and conclusions—around events, ideas, and even potentials! Is there a potential that humanity will end? Of course! But when you then create those scenarios that will support that idea, you also create a finite boundary around the potential that can then become a belief. Will that belief make that event happen? Not unless the consciousness of each of the elements involved in this perceived event is also lined up with it.

This is not healthy. Humanity is and always will be!

M: There is a prediction, although not mainstream, that around the year 2047, the sun will undergo a macronova event that could wipe out the Earth and every living thing on it. The patterns of history are being used to draw this possibility.

AR: Let us consider right now where humanity stands in its evolutionary development. Globally, there is much division, perhaps some perceived chaos and destruction occurring, all evolving from a collective fear. It is quite natural that there would be information arising about the end of humanity or of Earth herself when you consider the energy of fear. Fear looks for evidence of itself. It is on a continuous mission to find proof of its relevance. Fear has a desire to lock in an individual or group of individuals to further its existence.

Looking at the history of your planet, from what you can gather and understand, remember that these kinds of events have been perceived by your scientists and known specialists. The idea that the dinosaurs were wiped out in a blip of a moment may be different from what you have concluded. People from every time period in your history perceive, interpret, and make conclusions about events that have taken place before them, from the energy they are in in their present time. Therefore, the writings and other known evidence from past time periods in your history were written from the perception and nuances of that exact time period. No two people will interpret the same event in the same way. Our question to all of you is this: Does it really matter what happened eons ago? The most powerful place you can be is in the now. It is from the now that you can pre-pave your future and the future of the planet. History can trip you up. Did certain events really occur? Most likely, much of it did. And have you learned from some of these historical times? Of course, to some degree.

Back to the sun. Did the sun, thousands of years ago, emit a supernova event that wiped out sections of the planet? Only Gaia can answer that, as she holds the truth and knowledge of all that exists and will exist. However, your planet today is steeped in an energy of fear. And when one looks at history from this place, the conclusions and scenarios will translate into fear-based potentials. This is what is occurring around the sun's activity that is being predicted and spoken about at this time.

Today, humanity not only fears the future but fears the now. There is growing evidence that people operating in their now are gathering more fear-based ideas and attracting people to create fear-based potentials in the now. We cannot emphasize enough the importance of going inward in your now moments and allowing the light of each of you to speak directly to you. Try to listen quietly. At first, the thoughts that are associated with the density of your lives or your perception of a chaotic planet will flood your mind. That is fine. Allow them to drift by and away. We promise that eventually you will experience another sensation, another dimension, one of peace and light. And at this moment, know that this is you. It is who you are. You are the emanation of your own Divine, and the living, breathing essence of God/Source.

M: Does the sun have its own Akashic Records? And can I access them?

AR: The sun does have its own Akashic Records, and yes, you absolutely can access them. And we encourage this. Every living thing is etched in the Akashic Records. There is so much information and enlightenment available to humanity through the voices of living, breathing frequencies of consciousness that are inherently contained in all things on your planet, including the planet herself, other planets, and the galaxies!

M: It has been suggested that by raising our consciousness, we will have the ability to leave our planet or leap from it to another planetary home. Is this possible?

AR: Everything and anything is possible. Remember that when you are all thinking about leaping onto another planet, you are thinking of it from your third-dimensional reality. Once you raise or expand your consciousness beyond your third-dimensional reality, you will be able to shift, leap, visit, and travel anywhere in the cosmos. Many of you, when discussing this possibility, are assuming that there is another planet just like your own Earth, and you can simply continue living there as you are now. There is no other planet like Earth. There are areas in the galaxies where there are similar components to life on Earth, for example, specific gases, or oxygen, or water, but they do not exist in support of human life. Their roles are different depending on the planet or region itself. Let us shed some light on what it means to expand your consciousness. This term gets tossed about much lately. When a human meditates so deeply that they are no longer aware of their bodily form, this is a form of consciousness expanding. Now, imagine being in this state all the time. Most would agree that this might mean you are no longer a body, yes? This is true. Although while you are in this elevated state, others in the room will still see you as a form, sitting in a chair, your being, your spirit, has left. In this advanced state of being, one can travel and visit anywhere one chooses. So, you see, you need not wait until what you term the end of the world in order to visit elsewhere. However, it is critical that you develop a practice of leaving your body through this kind of deep meditation. Once you develop this, you can choose any place you wish to visit, for example, a planet, or somewhere in the cosmos, or maybe even the center of Gaia? As mentioned earlier, you can intend a visit to the other dimensions. You can remote-view or bilocate. It is all possible and all depends on your ability to release your connection to the third dimension where your body resides. If and when you practice this, then whatever earthly event occurs, you will already be versed in the how and where to transition to, or you may decide to stay on Earth. Your soul's chosen journey will reveal itself to you, and you will know, especially in this expanded version of you. This is exactly what raising consciousness is about.

The planet's consciousness will expand when enough people expand their own consciousness to these elevated states that we are speaking of. This collective expansion will, in turn, expand your planet. This will become evident when you experience and witness more loving acts of kindness throughout humanity.

This Akashic exchange reminded me that our deepest fears often arise when we feel powerless, but the Records gently revealed the opposite: We are infinitely powerful. The future of Earth is not fixed. It reflects our collective consciousness. Rather than dwell on projected cataclysms, we are being called to deepen our spiritual practices, raise our vibration, and step into our role as co-creators. The Akashic guidance was clear: There is no end—not in the way we have been taught to expect. Earth is not as fragile as fear suggests. She is an evolving consciousness, as are we. And the more we live from our expanded state of being, the more we align with the truth: All is well, and we are eternal.

THE SUN SPEAKS

THIS CHAPTER IS unlike any other in this book. Everything in existence—every living being, every soul, every planet, even the sun—has its own Akashic Record. With that understanding, I opened the Akashic Records of the sun, seeking to better understand the growing narratives about solar activity and Earth's future. What I did not expect was how distinct the energy would feel. I was accessing the Masters, Teachers, and Loved Ones of the sun itself, the radiant voice of Helios. What follows is a rare transmission from the Divine consciousness at the center of our solar system.

M: I am honored to be having this exchange with you, Helios, our great Sun.

SUN: Yes, I, too, am interested in this exchange. Humanity does not address me in this way. In the past of your planet, humanity did converse with me. It was wonderful because humanity and I are in co-creation. We all are. As your Earth progressed through the eons of years and time (as you know it), mankind began to distance itself from me. And in distancing itself from me, mankind began to create all sorts of scenarios about my origin, my role in the present earth-time, and my future.

M: I could hear you wanting to communicate from the Akashic realm.

SUN: Yes, because it is here in the Akashic Realm that all truth exists. What questions do you have for me? Let us begin here.

M: It appears that many predictions are pointing to your having a macronova event sometime in our near future, around 2047. Can you shed light on this?

SUN: Shed light? That is my forte! Of course! The only power is the now. I have been around for quite some time. I have gone through periods of unrest, periods of being tired, and a substantial number of periods of joy about my role in the entire Universe! I have a self-correcting Divine machinery within my core that recalibrates my entire being every so often. Your scientists are measuring future probabilities based on past patterns, or I should emphasize that your scientists look for patterns. If you look for a pattern, you will inevitably find one. That is the nature of the Universe. The Universe is loaded with patterns and textures, past, present, and to come. There is no such thing as random. But to equate a pattern with a future event is a waste of time. I am moving about and recalibrating at a rate you all are not capable of calculating. It is part of my power.

I am here to hold the Universe together, in a sense. Source created me to nurture and to have the ability to wipe out or extinguish non-light forces—and this I do. So, while I nurture the Earth and all other planets in your solar system, I am also eliminating darkness, which, of course, is my innate nature.

I am in service to the Divine All-That-Is. And I am the All-That-Is, too. We all are. Regarding Earth at this time in your history, God/Source is sending multitudes of Divine beings to your planet to assist in rebalancing it. I am part of this plan.

There may come a time when I will need to fully eliminate darkness on Earth. Let me explain. My key role is to extinguish anything non-Divine, or perhaps I should use the term trans-mute into light. You see, not all non-Divine entities and living things understand that to allow itself to transmute into light is the nature of life itself. Many are stuck in the false hypnotism of the dark itself. Gaia is participating greatly in this time of rebalancing. She is hurling storms, tsunamis, volcanic erup-tions, and other phenomena directly into humanity. This is a giant wake-up call. During these events, watch how masses of people gather in community to help one another. The truth is, if humanity were actually engaged in this community of com-passion and love for one another, Gaia would not be stepping in as she is. She is presenting opportunities for love through these events. Some might say this is an angry act for Gaia, but no, dear ones. She knows all. The souls of those who transi-tion during these events have agreed before incarnating to participate in these grand acts of love and compassion. It is an amazing outpouring of love for humanity—that certain souls choose to come to Earth for this reason.

Back to me. I have been emitting what you term "sun storms" from time to time. This is intentional. It is not be-cause something is becoming unbalanced in my gravitational fields and core, as some scientists conclude. I am throwing some powerful signals to your planet. You have allowed the collective ego to run the show, so to speak. This is not in line with Divine and its plan for the Universe. I have the power to throw off or disempower the entire collective ego. I can-not do that because that would be intervention without being asked. However, there are many lightworkers on your plan-et who know me and my role and are speaking with me as you are now. There is a strong possibility that I may disrupt your power grid. This, of course, will cause imbalances with-in your infrastructures. But those infrastructures have become extremely dangerous for humanity. Some of you know what I am referring to. Humanity is misusing technology for its own benefit. It may not be necessary for me to do this. However, I am keeping a watchful eye on humanity as it progresses through a shadow-based time period.

All will be well, please know this. Those who are connected to their inner Divine and who know that there is a God/Source who is co-creating with us will be guided to be in the right places on your planet if a grid event happens. Your scientists will blame me and will analyze that I am losing my balance and that my surface is expanding while my core does not, and that my core is firing explosions that will eventually throw my balance off. It has been predicted by these scientists that in four to five billion years, I will be a giant red ball in the skies and will cease to exist as your sun.

Please do not worry yourselves with these kinds of predictions. What matters is the now. Talk with me often. We are co-creators. I am not running the show. We are running this Divine show together. I love humanity. I love the Earth and every living organism that moves about, on, and within her. I ask that humanity begin to view me as a sibling. We are here for the same reasons. I do not like it that people are frightened of me. I realize my strength but look how strong humanity is! It is so strong that it can destroy itself! Look at my strength! I use it for good, to further the Divine plan to participate in an endless expansion of love and compassion throughout eternity. Communicate with me on this level, and I will help all!

To clarify a few things . . . I do not cause cancer. I have healing properties that you have yet to discover. Look to the journey of your plant kingdom to discover this. The plants know who I am. Also, I am not turning from yellow to white as many are saying these days (I was always white!). I am not going to turn my back on the Universe and destroy everything. I would and could have done this by now. I am billions of years young!

M: Do you have a sound that is your signature?

SUN: I do have a sound or frequency. Look into this. There are many who are identifying many sounds that I may have. But there is only one. Your scientists are using instruments created by man to determine my sound. This will not work. Oh, you will hear things and see various newer frequencies, but these are the result of your technology you are using, mixing or interfering with my true sound or frequency.

M: How can we discover or experience your sound?

SUN: I invite every one of you to be in silent meditation—no music, no sounds—just ultimate silence. Do this under me and in my presence. Let my energy flow through you and then speak with me. We can have conversations like we are now having. Ask me to reflect to you my frequency. It may not be in the way you expect. Be open! I will guide you to eventually hear me and my sound.

M: This is beautiful, as are you, dear Sun, dear Helios.

SUN: I love my name, Helios. You are feeling this, yes?

M: Yes, I do feel you more strongly when I think of Helios.

SUN: That is who I am. I play an especially significant role in the Universe. When God/Source created me, we had an ethereal exchange about what my role would become and how I would participate in a huge balancing act for Earth and all Universes. I accepted this because of my love of God/Source.

If you think my light is huge, you all should see the light of God/Source! Amazing!

Come to me often, my dear ones. I need you all as much as you need me. We are balancing everything together, and together we will eradicate all darkness, which by this I mean, all that is not of the Divine.

In Light and Love,

Helios

During this Akashic exchange, Helios moved through me with an unexpected warmth—not only of temperature but of presence. It was deeply personal, almost familial. I had never thought of the sun as a sibling or as a being with memory, compassion, and a Divine role in our cosmic co-creation. But now I do. This exchange reminded me that everything alive holds consciousness and that even the most powerful forces in our solar system are in sacred dialogue with us if we quiet ourselves long enough to listen. I hope that many will come to know the sun not as something distant or feared, but as an ally—guiding us back into balance in a co-creative dance.

EARTH IS SHIFTING—SO ARE WE

OVER THE COURSE of six years, I opened my Akashic Records to better understand the intensifying sense of chaos and imbalance I felt—both within myself and in the world. Though each exchange came in a different year and under different circumstances, the messages remained strikingly consistent: Earth is undergoing a massive rebalancing, Gaia is speaking, the light realms are responding, and we are being called, repeatedly, back to our Divine centers.

M: I find myself deeply exhausted—spiritually, emotionally, and physically. Something feels off, not just in me, but in the world.

AR: We reflect to you that you are not only tired, but you are experiencing all that is happening on and off planet. It is a very dense time right now. Everything is being squeezed into one ball of chaotic energy. It is because ascension is happening on so many levels.

M: Why do I feel so lost in my life right now? I can't seem to get centered.

AR: There are master changes and recalibrations occurring on your Earth plane at this time. Sensitive people will experience this in a greater way. You must be patient. It will pass. There has been an emergency of sorts on your Earth at this present time, and there have been interventions occurring to right the wrongs, so to speak.

M: What kinds of problems are happening to warrant non-physical interventions?

AR: Because your Earth has been ruptured in so many ways and at so many points, there has been a release of deep energetic fields from beneath her surface. These energy fields can be disruptive to human life. The interventions are dissipating the effects of this by sending a different kind of nonphysical energy into the problem areas. As this work is occurring, humans are feeling wildly off-center.

Because the Earth is shifting so fast, thought forms are no longer familiar—because newer ones are emerging at lightning speed. You are searching for your old thought forms, and they are no longer there. Allow the newer ones to come into your being and expand there. This in-between period is a difficult one—because you cannot find the old ones and you cannot see the new ones yet. That is why we want you to be patient right now.

Two years later, in another Akashic exchange, they again addressed planetary concerns:

M: I would like to know about what kinds of times are ahead for us here on Earth. Can my Records shed light on this?

AR: Yes, we can, as long as the information we send you is in line with your present soul's journey.

There will be catastrophes, and you will play a leading role in carrying people through them. Earth will continue to react to mankind's abuses. She is tired and frustrated and will be speaking her truth. That is what these catastrophes are all about. Mother Earth is speaking her truth. She has not been seen or heard for her Divine beauty for some time now, and she will be screaming out in horror. It has already been happening to some degree. Lightworkers have been going through a preparation for these times. There was a time when the catastrophes could have been averted, but you have passed that period.

M: What about nuclear accidents?

AR: We do not want to speak of this because it will veer you away from your soul's journey. We will speak of this at later times. Know that you and your closest dear ones will be well, but the future times will be challenging for humankind. This time period in the world and in the Universe is one of immense Universal cleansing. In a third-dimensional way, dark and light will cancel each other out, and what will remain will be a love energy that you cannot yet conceive. It will be a world never seen or written about yet.

Four years later, again concerned about the recent chaos on our planet, I asked for clarity.

M: What is happening on our planet today?

AR: Lots happening. Perceptions are running rampant. You are at a pivotal point in your Earth's history. Lightworkers have been summoned, both human and nonhuman, in a massive flood of love—love of each other, love of planet, love of animals and nature. Those disconnected from their Divine are working even harder to maintain power, but there is no power in a human who is disconnected from Divine. Not possible. Gaia is helping immensely—through weather changes, earthquakes, floods, in a massive balancing act. Balance will happen—not without those souls who have decided to transition. Many have transferred themselves back to the Divine Realm.

It is all good, as they will be needed greatly when they reincarnate. Trust that this is all one huge Divine choreography.

M: How can people be soothed?

AR: Love . . . more now than ever. As we have communicated earlier, the love we refer to is the love that resides in each of you. The planet is steeped in disguises of all forms and kinds. The collective ego has gotten hold of the idea of love, but that is not real. The best way to determine whether the love is real or not is to listen carefully to what your inner being says about it. When you think (with your mind) that something or someone outside of you is coming from love, take a moment and listen. Call on the love inside you to speak to you, to tell you what is and what is not real. From that place only will you be able to determine whether the people and forces outside of you are truly operating in the light of love.

M: I just heard a series of commercials on my television, and they were so offensive to me in this Akashic space.

AR: Yes, those are prime examples of the collective ego disguising itself as objects, things, and experiences that you think you may need or want. They are designed to magnetize watchers to their messaging. These marketing tools are often not coming from love. They are operating from a need-and-greed energy and base their successes on consumers falling prey to their supposed caring and offerings. This is ego-trickery, created by those who have not experienced their Divinity.

M: But not all commercials are bad, are they?

AR: We do not think they are bad. They are simply operating from manipulation energy. Think on this. Commercials base their messages on the idea that you need what they have, and a more subliminal message that you are not complete without what they have to offer and sell. This is not real. Humans have everything they need. Look to your past histories, and you will see evidence of this over and over. People have thrived through all perceived disasters and catastrophes. We say perceived because these events are simply emphasized energy manifesting into a state of imbalance. Too much energy put in one specific place causes a tip to occur. And that tip may be in the form of Earth events and human events. Disease forms from too much energy or no energy being given to one area. The areas of the body where there is less energy being given call out for help in the form of what you refer to as disease. All imbalances are beautiful signs to send more care, attention, and love to that area.

We encourage you all to turn off your televisions and devices as much as possible and spend more time in nature. Spend time listening to the sounds of nature. Talk to the trees, to the plants. Run your hands along a green bush and thank it for its life force. And when you feel the love from your planet, smile and know that this is exactly what you are made of. This is a mirror of the essence of you.

And now, again, I have brought my concern about the state of the world to my Akashic Records:

M: How can we navigate this world of such division and confusion, filled with fear, hate, and disheartenment?

AR: Stand together in the essence of the new Earth. There is no action necessary regarding the old world. It exists and will always exist in its own vibratory state, or timeline. Simply take a gentle sidestep to the right of it. That is how to release what no longer is a match to your new Earth. You see, this new

Earth is not really new. It always existed. You have evidence of this throughout your history. If you look, you will see an unlimited number of humans who were viewed as operating outside the box. They were called anomalies, geniuses, prodigies, as if they were different in some way. We would like you to understand that what is at the center of all is the reality of one humanity, steeped in love and compassion. It has merely appeared as if that reality does not exist. Dear ones, it has always been there. It is the design of Divine. Humanity lost touch with its inner reality, which is that it is only love. Over time, many have taken a step away from this whole, complete oneness. The massive collection of more and more people in that unreal space is where you all stand at this time in your history. However, the core of every human knows that what is real is love and light.

Imagine this scene: a man is rendered unconscious from an event. When he regains consciousness, he finds himself in the middle of a storm or a war, where what feels like chaos and harm abound. It is foreign to him. He cannot comprehend it. That man will immediately assess the situation in a split second and pivot into what you refer to as survival mode. However, that is not what is happening. The need for survival is an ego-created state of being. In the exact moment this man becomes conscious, he realizes that where he is is not who he is. His higher self emerges to usher him back to his own light. Now, imagine your entire planet in this situation at the same time. This is what is occurring. Humanity is opening its eyes (becoming conscious), becoming magnetized to its true reality. And you are all feeling it. The world you are opening your eyes to on a daily basis is not a true reflection of Divine design. It is an illusion created by the collective ego. What you all are navigating through at this time is not real.

Divine design is the one and only reality that exists. When you remember this on a deep level, the gentle sidestep we referred to earlier will be effortless. And actually, it is in the remembering of your true soul identity that you will find yourself already there. We call it home.

What I have come to understand through these exchanges is that—even now—we are living through a profound planetary rebalancing. We are part of this rebalancing because each of us has chosen to be on this planet at this time. The messages I've shared from the Akashic Records over the years point not just to global disruption but to a deeper call for individual responsibility and remembrance. We are not separate from the Earth's shifts—we are active participants in them. Whether we feel off-center or fully aligned, we are each being asked to return to inner stillness, to become conscious stewards of our own energy, and to choose love, even when it is difficult. We may not control the pace of change, but we can decide how we respond to it. The more we listen inwardly, the more we can see what is real, what is needed, and what our role is in this rebalancing.

THE DIVINE SPIRAL

WHAT IF IT'S NOT time that's speeding up, but rather us? This exchange with the Akashic Records reveals a vast and living truth—that humanity is moving not through a straight line of progress but through an ever-ascending spiral of Divine energy. As we cycle through this spiral, again and again, we do not repeat—we evolve, accelerate, and expand. We are not alone in this movement. Unseen forces—both light and shadow—are active in our world. But at the center of it all is a unified field of love, drawing us upward, inward, and ultimately together.

AR: We are all the same, and we are all reflections or mirrors of the same master Divine source of power that rotates the Universe in perfect synchronicity, forever. It is such a beautiful dance. There is never a beginning or an end. You advance and start and advance and start and advance and start, but there is no time in this dance. How can there be when you are traveling in a circle? But you see, each time you spin in this circle of life, you accumulate more energy, so your vibrational rate increases. This is why you feel like your time is moving faster. It is not. Earthly time is still moving at the same rate it always was. You, as a race, are trying to interpret the feelings you have of your beings moving faster. They are! As you move through eons of time within these master circles of energy, your vortexes move higher and higher—all of you, together, as one giant vortex of humanity. As you rise higher and higher, you begin to come together at the top, as in a pyramid. This is why it appears that more of you are connecting. You are . . . at the top!!

M: What will happen when we, as humanity, reach the top?

AR: You will begin to expand like a mushroom. We are looking for a picture that will depict this that does not seem comical or trite. But you see, this explosion of Divinity will feed back into itself and expand to create the next wave of Universes. It will explode outward into the galaxies and permeate your Earth plane at the same time. It need not be a catastrophic event. This explosion is already beginning to happen and is being evidenced in so many ways. Your 9/11 event was one. There will be more. This is a huge cleansing, like a giant washing machine tossing and turning at lightning speed into one explosion of love. This love will ripple down into your Earth and out into the spheres of the Universe. This is the meaning of your 26,000-year cycle. The reason so many nonphysical entities have re-emerged on Earth lately is because they are participating in the event and are here as guides as well. They are the buffers for you all, as the spinning gets more intense. By spinning, we mean the accelerated rate at which the energy is turning. Remember, it is humankind that is causing this to happen—a natural response to each individual's calling and the reason each individual is here at this precise time in history. Many of you have been here over and over and will continue to re-emerge on the physical plane. There are actually not as many of you as you think. From the beginning of time to your present time-space—time in your sense—there have actually only been a handful of you, even though there are billions of human beings now living on your planet.

Think about this: What if you all share the same soul? Then there would be only one human being, right? However, there are actually seven soul groups on Earth, and there are billions of beings, including animals and plants, who are part of one of these seven soul groups or energy streams. Each time you reincarnate, you come into one of these seven soul groups. You re-emerge with added expansion. Incarnating creates the expansion. This is why your Earth has been improving as your time moves on. But what is now happening is that those seven soul groups are merging. It is happening because the expansion is reaching a peak point—the point at the top of the pyramid of Divine power. You are approaching the one-soul state, a state of total unity and the point in which you will participate in the mushroom effect—and spin inward and outward at the same time. We know this is much for you to grasp, but it will make more sense when you share and reread this information. Humankind is about to become the original "one" that it was when Source first launched this grand scheme of humanity.

M: And then what will happen?

AR: You see, it has already happened! This is a play, or performance, or illusion of the All-That-Isness that has and will always exist. Just like every theatrical performance of the same play can change or evolve, but it continues to be performed, so is the journey of humankind. There is not and will never be an end to the performance or play of humankind. It will keep getting more expansive and faster (energetically speaking). When your plays in the theaters of your Earth are repeated, they continue to get better and better. They do not get worse. You may interpret them in a worse way each time they are performed, but they are not—they are always improving. This is the way of humankind: expansion, new, better, expansion, new, better, faster, explosion, expansion, new, better—all spinning around one giant force field—love. Do you get it?

M: I absolutely understand this, and it feels so good. I feel a vibrant, deep joy!

This spiral we are in is not chaos—it is choreography. We are spinning faster, yes, but with purpose, called into the top of a great pyramid where the illusion of separation dissolves. The Akashic Records remind us that we are not fragments. We are reflections of a single Divine Source, looping ever upward in collective remembering. And the next leap is not somewhere far away. It is already in motion. We are not waiting for it. We *are* it. This is the pulse of creation. This is the Divine Spiral.

DEATH

EVEN WITH ALL I've learned working in the Akashic Records—and even after connecting with my loved ones who have crossed over—I still find myself afraid of death, especially after many recent losses: beloved pets, dear friends, and most recently, my father-in-law. I asked the Records about it—not from a place of curiosity, but from a very human place of grief, uncertainty, and fear. What came through was not poetic or distant. It was simple, direct, and powerful. It reminded me that fear of death is not really about death itself. It's about our resistance to letting go.

M: Why am I so afraid of death? I understand that we continue on, and earlier in this book, I had a life-changing exchange with my loved ones on the other side. But I still have this fear around the idea of death.

AR: Mary, we assure you that there is no such thing as death, not in the way humanity expresses its relationship with it. Death implies an ending. There is no such thing. Maybe it will help you to change the word death to re-beginning. You see, that is exactly what it is.

The fear of death is entangled with the physical transition from the third dimension to multi- and/or no dimensions. This perceived fear has also created itself from those who are resisting the release into nonphysical, and therefore, they experience pain and discomfort. Are they really experiencing pain? Most likely, yes. But that has nothing to do with transitioning. The pain or discomfort is due to the resistant energy. Resistance is not a part of transitioning. It cannot be. Resistance is the ego-mind resisting being pulled from its connection to the human. Once that separation happens, the ego can no longer exist—its greatest fear! So, that little tug-of-war between ego and Divine becomes felt or observed by the human going through their transition. And when this is observed by others around that individual, the event may be interpreted as pain and suffering.

Once one transitions, they become immersed in pure Divine light.

M: How can we shift these negative perceptions around death?

AR: Keep shining a light on those beautiful, positive transitions by telling the stories of them. Have you noticed that there are so many more near-death experiences (NDEs) happening? These people who have experienced leaving and returning have chosen these events to shine a light on the natural beauty of the process itself. Their vivid descriptions of how they experience moving from physical form into no-form are so magnificent and so right-on. Their commitment on a soul level to engage in the process of a temporary transition is wonderful. They are the wayshowers of the reality that there is no death. Notice how they have no fear around death after they return. How could they, when they stepped into the beauty and reality of the essence of Divine love?

This exchange softened something in me. It didn't take away the ache of loss, but it gave me a clearer understanding of what death is and what it is not. Death is not an ending. It is not suffering—it is a re-beginning, a return to what we are at our core. The pain we feel is often just the ego letting go, and what comes next is light. The more we share this truth—through stories, through our own experiences—the less alone, and possibly the less afraid, we all feel.

CHALLENGES WITH
BUSINESS PARTNERS

I WAS STRUGGLING WITH a few of my business partnerships at this time and asked for clarity around my issues. I was feeling out of sync with their ideas and their responses to my ideas. I often felt mismatched with them, so I opened my Akashic Records to understand why I felt this disconnect. What emerged was a powerful teaching on the illusion of separation, especially within business. What I received was both validating and expansive. It reframed how I view business relationships—not as transactions, but as sacred collaborations.

M: I am having challenges with my business colleagues, who are also friends of mine, around ownership of ideas and how monies will be divided among us. It has created a tension that is interfering with why we first came together on this project.

AR: In love, there is no fear, no mistrust, no separation, no worries. In your physical world, you often make the mistake of separating; in fact, you state it over and over—separating business from friendship. They are one. Business is not separate from love. When you are in love of one another, all is always the same. It is the ego that searches for differences, justifications, and protections from being taken advantage of or not valued, which are often associated with business relationships. The perfect synchronistic groupings in humankind have been those that saw no borders . . . none. This can be hard for you because of your programming. You have been programmed through the field of fear to create division and separate ideas that you believe belong only to the one to whom it came. Do you now realize that all ideas that are strong, positive, and Divine come from the same place? It is the place of the Divine. Humankind will continue to expand to the top of the pyramid that we spoke of earlier when these business borders disappear. Mary, you have always been wanting to express and live out this scenario and have been frustrated when others label you a bad businessperson. You are not. You are coming from a time when there were no divisions. We speak of the time when your Jesus lived. Yes, there were wars, egos, but the grouping you were merged with traveled as one unit. Everyone respected everyone in the same manner and shared everything in the same manner. You are used to this. Many cannot see this yet.

So, we suggest that each of you take the human time to visit the Divine Realm, if you can. Whether through meditation, walking, communing with your pets, or simply doing nothing. Turn off your minds and you will see the solution. We guarantee this. Remember, this is material-minded stuff. It has nothing whatsoever to do with the roles you have all chosen and what lies ahead. We also guarantee you that each one of you will be taken care of. That is a given. You already have been shown that, yes? You will be taken care of whether you figure this agreement out or not. We know this sounds strange to you, but it is so. You are being guided by such an amazing power. Figuring out who gets what in the scheme of the business has absolutely nothing to do with anything. We hope you will see this. You all must relinquish fear and ego in order to resolve it and move on. If you choose to not relinquish fear and ego, then you will be living in a lie inside yourselves, because you all agreed to use the Divine parts of yourselves to fight this fight. Divine knows no fear, ego, divisions . . . no one is more deserving than another in the Divine. Your Earth plane is moving in this direction of realizing it. This is part of the expansion we have spoken of. You will not be successful in your partnership commitments if you do not stay in this space of love and equality. The more you remain in this field, the more people who want to be there too will join you. You have the head on you to ensure that equality equals love. Do not waver from it. We know how frustrated you get when those around you are over-worried about what they are getting versus others. These are exercises from the Universe designed specifically for you. We know how exhausting it is, and we see you are doing a magnificent job. Stay in it. You have been here before. Love does not lose—ever!

This reading revealed that the challenges I was experiencing were not signs that I was bad at business, but rather that I am wired for a more ancient, heart-centered way of working—one that transcends borders or hierarchies. My discomfort stemmed from being out of alignment with systems still rooted in fear and ego. I was remembering something older than this world's current business models—a time when communities were whole and every contribution was valued equally.

The Records affirmed that I am here to model that remembering and that when I stay committed to love, unity, and fairness without fear, I will naturally attract more partners aligned with those frequencies. This reading reminded me of a deeper truth: When we act from the Divine within us, there is no competition, no need for separation, and no scarcity—only shared purpose. Only love.

WHEN THE HEART RESISTS

As my work in the Akashic Records deepened, I discovered that not every reading flows easily, and not every client is ready to receive the profound truths being reflected to them. Early on, after a particularly challenging session, I turned to my own Records for clarity. What I received reshaped how I view this work, healing, and each soul's timing. I share this exchange because it captures one of the most important lessons of all: Divine truth is always available, but it can only be received when the heart is ready.

M: I just had a rather difficult reading with a client. I would like to understand why I manifested this.

AR: Let us begin, Mary. What was uncomfortable about it?

M: As I flowed the Divine messages, my client did not seem to let them in.

AR: She is in her own way. Often, this happens when people are unfamiliar with seeing themselves, for maybe the first time, from a soul perspective.

M: So, they put up a guard to not let in the info? I would like to understand more about when this happens. I sense that I will be encountering more of this because of the energies on the planet at this time.

AR: Yes. Exactly, Mary.

Let us explain more about what may have happened here. When people have established patterns that have brought them to what they think is a perfect life, they can become guarded from any new truths about themselves that can possibly be revealed. This can also become a mastery in protecting themselves (as a pattern) from ever being hurt in life—or at least that is what they have learned. When you have a need to protect, you emit an energy of that need, and those around you will show up to prove to you that you have a need to protect yourself. And it can keep going like this as long as you think you have to protect yourself in life.

But this is not Divine truth at all! There is never anything you need protection from. Everything is always a choice. That is it! When you are betrayed, it is because you are making a choice around the energy of betrayal.

Also, when people become steeped in financial abundance and have not worked out fully why they are here at this time, they can direct their abundance to protect them— and money cannot protect anyone! Add to this the learned state of mastery in competition, and you can drift farther and farther away from what is real, which is a deep love of oneself. It is important that humans come to know that the Akashic Records are not a prediction tool or a way to find out something new about themselves. The Records are a direct reflection of the deep, Divinely rich, unending essence of your souls. No one comes to the Records without their Records calling to them. The gift you have, Mary, is to help them see this.

M: But what if the client does not think they need to be reminded of who they are?

AR: Every human being who comes to visit their Records is coming because of an inner calling. They may not consciously realize this, but please know that this is one of the truths about the Akashic Records. A visit to the Akashic Records is never an accident or a mistake. That would go against the entire meaning and reality of the existence of Divine, the Akashic Records themselves, and what they represent on your planet.

M: I sometimes come away from readings feeling as if I have let the client down in some way.

AR: Mary, this is not possible. Through your Akashic work, you are allowing the Divine of each client to come through. You must trust that by simply intending to help others and by sharing your knowledge about the reality and power of the Akashic Realm, everything that occurs is always as it should be. Trust that Divine is handling all—all the time. Allow yourself to gently surrender into the arms of the Akashic Realm.

Now, regarding this earlier reading, you may have come up against a strong ego rearing up from this individual. This is the powerful trickery of the ego conscious. Remember that the ego fears its demise, and the Divine does not know or hold fear—it cannot because fear is not real. So, if a client is steeped in his/her ego consciousness, this will, in a sense, create a battle with the purity of the Divine. Ego knows that it is not real, and when it does, it ramps itself up. Ego does not know the heart, nor does it know the soul—it just thinks it knows itself. Its existence is based on it expressing itself on a constant basis. Did this reading feel like a battle of sorts?

M: Yes. Exactly. I kept hearing that she needs to let her heart run the show, and when I imparted that Akashic message to her, she jumped to third-dimensional things, events, explanations, and moved herself away from any discussion about her heart. It looked (to me) like there was an energy putting itself between her Akashic essence and her heart, and that energy was winning. It is interesting, too, that this individual thrives on competition.

AR: Yes, so her ego—which created the need for competition—puffed itself up more. But know this truth, Mary. Divine Power is all that there is. There is nothing else. Nothing!

M: So, let us look at this type of client who comes to the Records. She is a brilliant, intelligent manifester. She teaches others—specifically women—how to come to know their power. She gives to others on a large scale and is greatly connected to the animal kingdom, especially horses. She is a practicing psychologist and has mastery in competition.

AR: She may have a completed meal of third-dimensional accomplishments, but there can be, at the same time, a loss of self, a loss of a connection to her own heart. Often, when humans have not experienced the beauty of their heart centers, and we mean that they have not felt the completeness that comes with truly loving themselves without having to connect with anything outside of themselves, they can be tricked into thinking they are totally fine and that all is well. But upon a closer look, we will see that they are using their outer world to keep them from their inner heart centers. So, they channel all their masteries from this and past lives outward (in her case) in a really positive way. If they take the time, or a time out, to do nothing at all, they will begin to have an unfamiliar sensation. It will seem unfamiliar because they have been covering it up and running from it all of their lives. So, it can feel strange when they first encounter the power of their heart—without any connection to anything outside of themselves. This may have begun to occur this morning. And you may not have witnessed it. Divine is always working its magic!

M: Yes, she ran from it . . . had another meeting. And she mentioned that she did not learn anything new about herself.

AR: Aha! There it is again! Humans expecting that the answers about their lives come from outside. Not a chance! All answers reside inside every one of you, Dear Ones!!!

This experience taught me that every Akashic session unfolds exactly as it is meant to, even when it appears otherwise. We cannot force openings. We cannot rush the heart. Each soul arrives at its readiness in its own Divine time. My role is not to fix or prove anything. It's simply to hold the sacred mirror, to trust the perfection of the moment, and to honor the courage it takes for anyone to even seek the light of their own soul. Clients who seek Akashic readings do so because they are drawn to their Akashic Records. This has been my experience since beginning my Akashic Records practice. I have learned to surrender to the truth—that Divine is always at work, even when I cannot immediately see it. And this is interesting—my clients who have appeared uncomfortable or resistant in their readings quite often return to visit their Akashic Records again.

ETS/UFOS—ARE THEY HELPERS?

FROM THE MID-1980s through the 1990s, I had some profound, unexplainable experiences. At that time, there was no one in my life I could share them with, except my one dear friend Terrayne, who assured me that I wasn't going crazy. Years later, and especially today, the idea of UFOs and alien abductions is an accepted concept. I decided to seek clarity in my Akashic Records regarding why these visitations and experiences happened to me.

M: I am wondering about my past UFO/alien experiences and whether revisiting them can be helpful to me at this time.

AR: You are wondering if they truly exist, Mary? Yes, indeed. There are many races who are working to right the many wrongs on Earth. They came to you because you invited them, unconsciously. You do not remember your experiences in this way because your ego created a huge fear around them. This is why you cannot remember seeing them during the encounters. Many of these races are tools for connecting humans to God/Source. They function out of pure love. The new generation of humans who are incarnating onto Earth now are indeed from these races. They have chosen to guide Earth away from hate and fear into light. You and your Christine are correct to see this. We can help you, Mary, to decipher what you need from your past experiences. It will only become clearer if you write about it, as you journey back and forth to the experiences.

M: Why do UFOs seem so familiar to me?

AR: You have been with them before. They are your family. We know now that you are ready to accept this in your journey. They are your home. You had a deep sense of this many years ago, but then as you entered your ego phase, you began to misinterpret their agenda and your role in it. You came from a very advanced, telepathic race, Mary, and you chose to come here and embrace the human experience. Your encounters have been simply you reconnecting with your own ancestors to share the human experience with them. This agenda is especially important today because the more the technologically advanced races can learn about humans, the more they can help out on Earth. Have you noticed that there are increasing numbers of advancements in innovations that are presenting solutions to many of Earth's major problems—in health, in the environment? By these parallel races understanding humans, they can correctly choose from their own assets what will be useful for Earth. Part of this agenda has involved the taking of human DNA, and yes, creating hybrids, integrating them with humans who are now residing on your Earth plane. Mary, you are very tuned into being able to recognize these new hybrids. They are not always children. Very often, they are adults, and you recognize them immediately. Trust yourself when you sense this.

M: Will I be having more encounters with them—ones without fear?

AR: Most definitely, you will. Be calm about it. You will still experience the human fear that is associated with abductions.

They are placing you in a state of non-feeling for your journey, so know all is well, and these experiences will feel less heightened. You are travelling to them more than you know when you are asleep. There are now ways to visit them that do not involve such abrupt methods. You will know when you have been visited by them or visited them because you will awaken in the morning feeling very heavy, similar to when you have been swimming in water and step out of the water and feel your weight.

M: Can I journal my abduction experiences here, while I am in my Records? I feel safer doing this in this Divine space.

AR: We think this is a good idea because you will feel more comforted knowing we, your Divine entourage, are holding your hand. Listen carefully for our thought forms to help you decipher the meaning of the experiences. You are very experienced at noticing the difference between what your mind is creating and what we are conveying to you.

M: My first known experience was when I was about three years old. I was in my crib in my house. I remember a blinding ball of light coming toward me, and I screamed, "No!" I kept saying, "No, No, No!" It was so intense and so blinding to me. It really frightened me.

AR: Mary, it was a white light. Remember. Try to imagine that this was a good indication that you were being visited by a benevolent being. This was where you came from. They were revisiting you to assure you that you would always have them as your home.

You have often referred to your upbringing as "being in the wrong family, somehow feeling out of place." Yes, you have always been out of place. Remember, you are here with all of your experiences because your soul made the choice.

M: When I was little, and my mother took me shopping with her (I was in grammar school), I remember hearing a strange vibration in my ears and head. I would ask her what it was, and she would say, "What sound? I don't hear anything." I described it to her as "atmosphere," that I was hearing atmosphere. I pleaded with her to listen and hear that there was a high-pitched sound. She never heard it. She thought I was crazy, so I stopped telling her that I was hearing it. To this day, I often hear this atmospheric frequency, especially when I am working in the Akashic Realm.

AR: Yes, Mary, you have always been hearing other realms, other worlds—the vibration of parallel universes. Those shifts in your ears are the same thing. More humans are beginning to experience hearing the shift of the Universe.

M: Next, I remember being in grammar school or just starting high school and feeling scared that I had a brain tumor. I would feel sensations of being separated from my body in some way. I remember telling my mother that I felt weird. She never understood. I kept complaining about this strange feeling. I kept feeling, not dizzy, but slightly separated while moving about in my life. I convinced her to let me go to a psychiatrist and to have an X-ray to see if I had a brain tumor. It turned out that there was nothing wrong.

I am feeling intense heat and sweating right now. What is this?

AR: You are activating your connection to other Universes. Stay with it, Mary.

M: My inner ears are hearing the atmosphere . . . no other word for it.

AR: That is because there is no word for it . . . not your words. Type out what you are sensing, not thinking.

Shgut buied98 ##@) nuitr oiu0 njha skli vber cfter sdpo huid cbvs khwi thud shdgit sbgvcx troy sjio dhhie bhkdoe sjjbiwu buirbfj lskjl oioue s kklje sdel s wpppa iuiehr cbjnsbi hufhei99hj snjdw;ajks cnnjdope skkj;[aw ncir djnwwoa ndk spowj fn va klsk oe fjd dj iosp wpodn k fpe djp cnj fjoe k sl;a;a; fji fnvn-voenfja jpw dmksp

AR: This is light code, Mary. You can do this often. Take time after you close your Records to look it over. Try to say it. See what you get from it.

M: This feels crazy.

AR: This is simply your doubt. You do not need it anymore. What do you have to lose by not having doubt? Absolutely nothing!!

M: (Smiling) Yes, I see. I had several other experiences over the years, including being yanked backward through walls while asleep in various locations—once while visiting Ireland—plus episodes of missing time, sometimes alone and sometimes with others. I never remembered what occurred while I was "away," but I always recalled being taken and then returning to my bed. Many times I struggled to speak upon waking, with my partner having to shake me fully awake. In the days following these experiences, I always felt strangely off-kilter.

AR: Yes, this is what happens when traveling to other realms. We wish experiencers to know that in order for you to move beyond your third (solid) dimension, you must be "helped along" by being placed into a state where you will not experience the shift from your present form to a space of pure consciousness—a condition of "unsolidness." This is a state of not remembering. During these journeys, downloads of information, insight, and enlightenment are often given to experiencers.

M: This eases my discomfort around these encounters.

AR: Yes, this is a good thing for you. Do not be afraid to jog loose these experiences. You were clearly given something special during these encounters, and by revisiting them, you will have the opportunity to remember what was given and accept your role here on Earth at this time. This is all good, and we are here to assist you.

This exchange helped me reframe what I once viewed as frightening or strange. The Akashic Records confirmed that these experiences were not random. They were part of a larger relationship I have with advanced beings who are here to help and that perhaps I am part of them. What I had dismissed or doubted for years turned out to be a key part of my role on Earth. Revisiting these encounters in a safe, grounded way gave me the clarity to see them for what they were: connection, not confusion; support, not fear. And that insight continues to unfold.

This Akashic reading is also an example of how we can take anything we are experiencing in our lives, whether misunderstood or confusing, into our Akashic Records and receive clarity and understanding—never with judgment. Non-judgment is one of the three attributes of the Akashic Records: fear not, judge not, resist not.

AKASHIC CLARITY
FOR MY WIFE

THIS CHAPTER CONTAINS a sacred and intimate reading I did for my wife, Christine. With her permission, I include it here as an example of how personal the Akashic Records can be and how profoundly they speak to the heart of one's journey.

Christine asked about her health, her purpose, her past wounds, and the nature of our connection as a couple. What came through was powerful—an unwavering reminder that healing begins when we release the grip of the mind, and that love, in its purest form, is the medicine we have been seeking all along.

She and I hope that her questions and the answers she received offer insight for anyone struggling with uncertainty, self-doubt, or a feeling of disconnection from their own Divine knowing.

Christine: I want to know about my health. My first concern is about this dizziness that I have been experiencing. Is this a serious health issue for me?

AR: Christine, you are resisting so much right now. It is in this resistance that you will find all sorts of health issues. Remember that you took in a lot of ethereal information last night. This is a deep area of remembrance for you. You will be experiencing many shifts right now in your conscious state.

Be patient with it. We want you to know that if you can release this resistance, your health issues will all clear up.

C: Can you clarify what the resistance looks like for me?

AR: Most certainly. It is when you, Christine, try hard to make sense of things that absolutely cannot be clarified with your mind. You must let go of the urge to utilize your mind. The shifts taking place for individuals at this time in your world are profoundly serious. Most people are experiencing them. Try to spend time doing nothing at all—no computer, no television, no focus on the animals, no talking—nothing at all. We are not saying to meditate. We are saying to get in the habit of sitting still and doing nothing. Your mind will try hard to take you over. Let it! What will happen will be that it will have nothing to do, so it will eventually settle down; in fact, it will shut down. This is what we want for you.

C: Ok, I will, thank you. I was told that my chakras are closed. Is this true?

AR: They are indeed! You see, Christine, your mind has been telling you that you are "open and connected." When the mind gives you that idea, beware! To be connected needs no thought to tell that you are. You just are! When the awareness of you being "connected" comes in, you are actually disconnected. We ask that you not try to decipher what we are saying here. Just read on and let it "settle." Do not try to figure it out. There is a calm subtlety about being connected. When being connected with you, the Divine self can contain absolutely no thought.

M: Wow. I really get this myself.

AR: Yes, Mary. We want you to have this too. Remember, when you are thinking you are connected, you are not connected at all.

C: Yes, I get this. What about my physical health? Do I need to go to a doctor for what seems to be happening physically to me these days?

AR: Christine, really "tune in" to YOU. And listen to what you "feel." Again, do not think about it. Just listen to the very first impression you receive when you ask about your health. We repeat: the very first impression you receive. When you miss the first impression, then you are missing the solutions to everything. Even if there is a picture given to you as the impression, write it down. Feel it. Breathe it in.

We cannot tell you that you are sick. Because there is no such thing as sickness. It is a fabrication of humanity. Not there at all. This is the big secret that many have been keeping from many. There is no such thing as illness.

If you think you need outside help to feel better, then seek outside help, but we can assure you that your inner being, as reflected in your soul's journey here in your Records that we are guarding for you, is as pure as anything you could ever imagine. Pure essence. Bask in the love of life that you have, the love of animals that you have, the love of Earth that you have, and you will only feel wonderful all the time. Focus your energy outside of your physical self. Look around every day at the small, beautiful things that surround you. Take them in, feel them, and send love out to anyone you can think of who needs it. You can do this in your quiet time or when you are busy, too. We think it would benefit you if every time you find yourself feeling like a victim to your mind chatter, in that very instant, send love out from you. This will immediately cleanse your mind, body, and spirit, we promise.

Please try this, Christine. We will remind you of how different you felt after you were visiting with your friend who is ill, or we should say, your friend who thinks she is ill. You were clear—you were happy. You did not wonder if you were happy. You just were.

Regarding your health, there also may be an element you are lacking as you are engaging in your new way of eating. This is all good, and a match for who you are at this time on this planet. By your eating this way, you will become more valuable to others in the upcoming trying times. Your planet is quite polluted. It is also abundant, but very polluted. You will be the one who will save others. It is written in your Records. You are following your soul's journey very well, Christine. But know that although the foods you are eating are, in theory and in their original state, beneficial for you, they are not in that state right now, and they may be doing some harm to you. We ask that you take moments before ingesting your food and feel—do not think, but feel—the energy of the food. There will be times that you may have a sense that you are not to eat what you have prepared. You must be in touch with your food on a Divine level.

There is an imbalance of nutrients in your body. A naturopath would be helpful for you to discover how to restore balance through proper eating habits. We want you to know that you are making good mental choices, based on your research, your readings, and your information that you are ingesting. But remember that you are using your mind to decide what to eat. We suggest that you use your intuition instead. Let go of the connection to being vegan. The term vegan is an idea. Your connection to this idea can be getting in your way of seeing the proper balance of foods you need. We are not saying to not eat in a vegan way. You are meant to revere animals, and that means not ingesting them into your being. This is a beautiful part of who you are. But there are some things you will discover you need more of. Your journey is to discover these.

C: Are there foods that I should be avoiding?

AR: No, not avoiding, but perhaps changing the time you eat. And try to begin your day earlier. Begin taking in food earlier in your day and completing your last meal earlier as well.

We want to suggest that you have an awareness, a sensation about the healthiness of the foods. Even organic foods are not necessarily healthy. Besides the obvious use of chemicals in your foods, even the organic ones, you must realize that there is energy in the foods, and not always the God-energy that the foods began with. Because of the greed of businesses that sell food, even organic ones, that energy can mar the food. So, get in the habit of blessing the food before eating it.

C: Is there anything else that I can do to feel better?

AR: We have covered much here. We do not want to overwhelm you, Christine, because you are serious and could get bogged down in the words of the reading. Try to laugh more and relax.

Again, quiet your mind. It is important today more than ever to pay attention to your intuitive feelings. The shift in energy patterns on your Earth today is confusing many. Some will get sick, some will transition, some will come in and leave before they take their first breath, some will wander about in a sleep-like state, and some will simply be in joy through it all. And Christine, trust in you. You need no one. No one. Allow yourself the time to learn the difference between thinking thoughts about who you are and knowing who you are. You are Divine—plain and simple.

There is no thinking required to figure any of this out. Just be.

And when you feel strange, embrace it, inhale it, welcome it, and know that you are always protected and guided by your guides and teachers.

You have much to accomplish still. And once you step outside of your thoughts, you will fly.

C: Dear Masters, Teachers, and Loved Ones, thank you for helping me. I appreciate it more than words can express! I LOVE YOU!!!

AR: Christine, we reflect back to you the love that is you. You are such a precious being. When we are having these interactions, remember that we are you mirroring you.

C: Thank you. I have a few more questions. First, was I a mind master in more than one lifetime? I feel I have been subconsciously struggling my whole life, torn between what I love to do—my passion—and finding a job to support my lifestyle, making me feel stuck and unaccomplished. Can you help me resolve this?

AR: When you are feeling stuck, it is because you are in the process of transforming past karma. Once this happens, you will be set free. You will feel it. Take a look at the things you feel confused about. If you are confused about anything, then it does not belong to you in this lifetime! It is truly that simple! Every time you wonder, "Why is this in my life?" . . . get rid of it!

C: Wonderful! Touching on past lives, was I ever instrumental in changing things on Earth in some way?

AR: You helped people feel strong in themselves. The one part of you that has been functioning lifetime after lifetime is your power. Your power is a deep one. In its raw state, it knows no judgment, no opinion. It just knows what truth is, what love is. When you relinquish your mind's hold on it, you will again access it as you did in the past. Your mind is jealous of this inner power. It wants to guide it, to show it how to act. But this power inside needs no guidance—it is rock solid. You have taken it through every lifetime, Christine. It has saved you from hurt, and it has shown others that they can do anything.

C: Wow, thank you. I recently won a photography session in a silent auction for charity, and I feel afraid to move forward with it. Can you help me remove this block? Are these photos part of my future path, or am I holding on to unfulfilled desires from the past and not willing to let go and move on?

AR: There is no block. You are unsure because you are disconnected from your inner self. We want to remind you that your desires from the past were fulfilled, not unfulfilled. If you are speaking of your past life as a well-known performer, you have been fulfilled over and over again.

We want to explain something about the human ego. The ego tricks you into thinking something is not good. There is nothing that is not good. You see, if the ego does not have anything to worry about, then it will not be needed. This is its greatest fear.

Your Records show you accomplishing absolutely whatever you have an inner desire for. So, there it is. There is no more. Go in, feel what feels good to you, send love outward continuously, and everything you desire will gently come to you, with ease.

C: That sounds so simple, but I have been told that I lack confidence when it comes to the things that I am passionate about, which has kept me from success. Can you help me with this?

AR: Our answer to you lies in this question; right at this moment, take a long, deep breath in and out, then ask yourself if you lack confidence. Then listen with love. The very first impression (not thought) you get is your answer. We know the answer, but you must receive it from within your Divine you.

C: I do not lack confidence. That does not even feel true to me at this moment.

AR: You see, when you listen to your first impression, that reflects your truth. We encourage you to recognize the difference between that inner minuscule moment and the mind (ego). Your mind (ego) was what constructed the question to begin with. Your ego encouraged you to connect your perceived lack of confidence with no success. But your truth is that you do have confidence, therefore, there is nothing in the way of your success.

C: Wow. That is such a relief. I can see now that there is nothing in the way.

AR: And know that there never was anything in the way.

C: Beautiful. There is another topic that I need clarity about, and that I feel very intense emotion over, which is the torture and abuse of animals by humans. Is this part of my journey in this lifetime? Can you help me understand my pain about the animals?

AR: Your pain is so very real, Christine. Yes, of course, this is your journey, which is why it runs so deep. You are experiencing the intense, deep love that you have inside you. This is why you are feeling it so much for the animals. Animals reflect love, always, so you see, when you are in their presence, you are experiencing that same love inside you that is you. So, the abuse of the animals is abuse to the deepest Divine part of you. As you begin to love your Divine you more, the pain will cease regarding what is happening to the animals. We are not saying that you will change your role in bringing others to learn to honor and respect them; in fact, you will become more powerful in taking actions that will help change the situation around the abuse of animals. Again, Christine, we hope you really let this settle in—the intense pain from the animal abuse is the intense pain you are carrying inside of you. Release your pain, and the sharpness around the animal abuse will loosen its grip on you, so you will then be able to help them.

C: Whoa, that is profound. What's the wound that I brought with me in this lifetime to heal?

AR: Self-loathing. Do not think about it. When you hear this word, feel into it. Christine, part of your journey today is to discover that you already have the answers inside of you. We think that sometimes it is not good to focus on past lifetimes, especially if the memory of them remains painful. The healthy use of past lifetimes is to allow the energy of them to transform into enlightened assets as you evolve and expand. As this happens, then you will be able to apply the energies of those lifetimes as part of the unfolding and manifestation of your soul's chosen journey in the now.

C: Is my grandfather, Eddie, one of my group of Masters, Teachers, and Loved Ones? When I am in the Divine space of the Akashic Records and I think of him, I feel very, very emotional, like right now. I feel him loving me. Is this real, or is it my love for him that I feel? When I asked this question, the intense emotion disappeared.

AR: He is indeed the love that you feel. He is with you always, and yes, he is part of your Akashic guides. The reason it disappeared was because you were thinking about the question. Just speak with him. He is always listening. You must summon him with love and then listen, and you will hear him, we promise. And this is true for all human beings who are wanting to connect with their loved ones on the other side.

C: Why did Mary and I come together in this lifetime? Are we soul mates? I had always considered myself heterosexual, but the energy between Mary and me when we met was undeniable—and confusing. If we are soul mates, why did she not come in as a man so our relationship would be easier for me to understand? Why have we had so much conflict between us over the years that made us fight? Are we preventing each other from being happy and successful?

AR: There is no one who can prevent another from being successful. Not possible. The only thing that can prevent one from following their soul's chosen path is the ego. You and Mary are part of the same soul group. This is why it was so easy to merge with her. You were already merged before this lifetime. If you were drawn to Mary, then there is no confusion. The confusion came as you were thinking about the world outside of yourself. You know that deep inside of you, love is all there is. Love does not choose or judge.

Please understand that individuals do not incarnate to make it easy on others. They come into a lifetime to evolve, grow, and add to the expansion of the Universe. Mary coming in as a woman in her time has more to do with her own expansion and evolution.

Much of your fighting was because you were both immersed in environments that were not a match to your souls' chosen journeys. If you did not deeply know and love each other, you would not be together at this moment in time.

You are both growing magnificently, individually and together. This is your time now, as you are both finding your paths—and discovering that you both share the same evolutionary path.

C: Can we delve deeper into the meaning behind my choosing my family? How have I greatly affected my family members? Since they cannot tell me, can we talk about it here, now? What is the healing that I have come to assist them with?

AR: Just by being born to them, Christine, you have already healed them. There are paths they might have taken that, by having you, they did not. You are a silent, powerful glue that holds them together. You may not see this in your outer world; however, know that this is true. We cannot delve into their lives, as that would be within their individual Records. But we show that you intentionally chose this family so that you would have compassion for others who struggle with very painful family situations.

C: Will there ever come a time when I can communicate with you directly?

AR: Of course you can! What is prompting this question? The answer to that is what is in the way. Move it aside, love your Divine you, and simply listen.

C: Thank you! I feel so much love right now! Communicating with my Masters, Teachers, and Loved Ones has been truly transformational. You've reminded me who I am and helped me see my life and the world around me—only and always—through the lens of love.

This Akashic reading reminded me that even when we walk this spiritual path together, each of us must find our own way home. Christine's questions were brave, honest, and full of longing, and the answers she received—about love, ego, intuition, and the body—are universal.

I was also reminded again that the Akashic Records are not a realm we visit to *learn* who we are—they are a place where we *remember*. Christine remembered that she is Divine; she is not broken, and she is not separate from the love she seeks—she *is* that love—all the time.

WHY ME?

As I approached the final pages of this book, one lingering question remained—a question that has lived with me for some time: Why is it that when I enter my Akashic Records, I receive messages not just for myself but for all of humanity?

This chapter is the response I received. It is the final piece in this sacred conversation—a reminder that the Akashic Realm is not only a source of personal healing but also a bridge to the greater Divine collective. As you read this final exchange, I invite you to reflect on your own purpose and your own capacity to receive.

M: Why, when I open my Akashic Records, am I continually being given not only clarity around my personal life but messages for humanity?

AR: Let us express clarity for you, Mary. You see, when you are working with others in their Akashic Realm—with their permission—you are immediately and continuously available for their highest good. Through your commitment to the light of the Records themselves and your intention to be of service to that person for their highest good, you are only going to, in a sense, stream their light to them. When you are in your Akashic Records, you are tapping into and reigniting the essence of you. Part of your soul's chosen journey for many lifetimes—especially this one—is to stand for and be a steward of the unending and ongoing presence of Divine Source. Your Records, dear Mary, contain your multitudes of lifetimes where you walked with God—in the form of relationships with those others who knew God. These accumulations of enlightened experiences, etched in the truth of the Divine, have evolved you into becoming an ascended master—one who has walked the planet over and over and participated in humanity's unfolding. You received information, knowledge, and enlightenment—through your interactions and from the angelic realms—about this Earth, the cosmos, and the purpose and meaning of the world as it unfolds its relationship with the Divine Realm. You have accumulated, in a sense, more wisdom from each lifetime. As we have imparted before, there is no time—but for the sake of understanding, we can express that there are layers upon layers of Divine learning you have amassed in this way. Think about what happens when you open your own Akashic Records.

M: I usually begin with a concern or feeling of being stuck about something in my life, and I bring it into my Akashic Records. My Records always shed clarity and understanding in a bubble of love and light. That is how I experience it.

AR: Right, and you are, right now, in your Akashic Records, yes?

M: Yes. Because I am seeking clarity around why I receive messages for humanity.

AR: Your Akashic Records contain everything you have experienced, in a sense, lifetime after lifetime. The information you have accumulated sits in the quantum energy of your DNA. When you enter your Records, you activate that quantum field that contains all that knowledge and wisdom, as well as all of your thoughts and actions from the past. It is with this mystical aspect of all versions of you that you have entered this lifetime—with a greater role than ever before.

M: But why am I only now coming to this realization about my role in humanity?

AR: Because you chose to first embody the experience of being a human in this lifetime—your growing-up time, your relationships, your perceived ups and downs, your joys, fears, and doubts—you are an experienced human being, Mary. Now, when you connect with the higher Divine Realm, you can encapsulate and impart this quantum Divine energy in a way that others can receive through their humanness. Do you see? You chose to bring your past connection with the Divine to the here and now. You have mentioned to others that this seems so easy for you, this experience of hearing the rumblings of the Divine. It is easy because you are simply remembering what you have already lived and experienced—the All-That-Isness of which we/you speak. Yes, a reminder here that WE ARE YOU ARE WE. You are tapping into an infinite stream of God/Source—Endless.

This reading was huge for me. I had, until this time, placed myself in more of a receiving mode, as if the information coming in was coming from somewhere outside of me. To be fair, I knew I had to have a deep connection to the Divine, and I have always known that I *am* Divine. However, I don't think I had fully acknowledged my role in humanity, as they have explained above.

I chose this reading for you because I am a living example of embracing courage and fortitude to accept my role and put it into action, fully acknowledging that this is a path I chose eons ago. I invite you to release any fear of your greatness. Embrace it!

CLOSING AKASHIC MESSAGE
FOR HUMANITY

AR: Dear Ones, at this present time, your world is on the pivot of full transition—from a space of non-light, non-divine into full awareness that you all are whole, balanced expressions of Divine love. As the Divine keepers of love and God/Source, we are here for each and every one of you. Know that you are courageous beings of light, who each chose to be here on your planet at this specific time—to assist in the grand design of one of the greatest expressions of Universal love. We will continue to mirror to you the reality of your role in this design, and we will be—and are to infinity—loving you over and over and over, washing you in your own magnificence so that you may emanate this vibration of reality out into the cosmos. Do not be afraid of how big it may seem. There is no end; there are no boundaries. There is only more and more of this powerful essence of light and love, and the best part is that you have the opportunity to acknowledge the grand beauty of this infinite love as you. It is you, dear ones. At this time in your world, gather together and join hands in solidarity—that this is what is truth.

We Love You to Infinity.

CONCLUSION:
A RETURN TO YOUR LIGHT

A s you close these pages, know this: nothing has ended. Something, I hope, has been reawakened.

This book is more than my personal story or even the voice of the Akashic Realm speaking through me. It is an invitation—one that reflects you, your longings, your questions, and your sacred path. Each message, each remembrance, was shared with the hope that it would stir something ancient and true within you, as it did for me.

I titled this book *The Akashic Way* because I believe that living life through the Akashic Records is a path back to ourselves—a way to remember who we are, why we chose to come here, and what we are here to do. When we view our lives through our own Akashic lens, we experience self-empowerment in the most profound way. The journey becomes less about seeking and more about allowing, remembering, and aligning.

The Divine is not distant. It is not above us or outside of us. It is alive within each one of us—a mirror of the Divine light from which we are never separate.

You may return to this book repeatedly. Open to any page and let the words meet you where you are. They will, as they still do for me.

As you continue your journey of remembrance, may you walk with greater clarity, strength, and a deeper trust in your soul's unfolding.

With love,

Mary

ACKNOWLEDGMENTS

I HAVE DEEP LOVE and gratitude for so many special friends and colleagues who have walked beside me throughout my life, held my hand, shared their wisdom, and offered me support about so many things that I could not understand at the time. You are all so beautiful and unique.

To Tammy Leech, whose steadfast friendship and deep belief in me offered the final affirmation I needed to walk the path of the Akashic Records. Your support has been a constant presence in my life, and your role in this journey is both meaningful and enduring. You are the sister I never had—my chosen family. Our connection is one of the greatest gifts in my life.

To my friend, colleague, soul sister, and publicist, Dea Shandera-Hunter. You saw my light from the moment we met. You have championed my voice and vision with a fierce, steady grace that has cleared the way for my work to reach further than I ever imagined. Your deep wisdom, generosity of spirit, and unwavering belief in the power of the Akashic Records continue to open doors for this work to be seen, heard, and felt. You are a remarkable friend, a powerful force, and a light on my path. I am so grateful for you.

To Terrayne Crawford. You occupy a sacred place in my heart—one that transcends time and lifetimes. Throughout our four decades of deep, soulful friendship, we have witnessed each other's evolution and nurtured a shared vision of a better world—one anchored in the light and love of God/Source. Your presence in my life is a gift beyond measure.

To Reverend Dr. Temple Hayes. You are a radiant beacon of light and a true force of Divine energy. Your unwavering friendship and continued support of me and my Akashic Records work have been invaluable. As a globally recognized spiritual leader, author, and humanitarian, your dedication to uplifting humanity is evident in every endeavor you undertake.

With gratitude to my cousin Lee Passarella, an accomplished artist whose extraordinary work graces this cover. Together we rose from the trenches of our past and made something of ourselves. Lee's strength and artistry continue to inspire me.

I am deeply grateful to my publisher, Susan Shankin, whose creativity, gentle nature, and gifted mastery made this journey both easy and joyful. Susan seemed to merge completely with *The Akashic Way*, infusing the process with her artistry and soulful alignment that allowed the book to unfold with grace.

My heartfelt thanks to my editor, Joyce Walker, who understood from the very beginning the depth and meaning of this book. Her editing skills, beyond expert, brought clarity and brilliance to every page.

And finally, to my Akashic Records clients. Thank you for answering the call to your Records with trust, openness, and courage. Each reading with you has deepened and expanded my own connection to the Divine Realm. Your willingness to remember who you are inspires and humbles me.

ABOUT THE AUTHOR

MARY MADEIRAS is an advanced Akashic Records practitioner, author, screenwriter, and three-time Emmy Award–winning television director whose career bridges two worlds—broadcast entertainment and spiritual transformation. For nearly two decades, she has opened the Akashic Records for individuals, couples, and corporations worldwide, offering soul-level insight that fosters clarity, healing, and success.

Her path to the Akashic Records began with a synchronistic encounter that ignited a calling. What unfolded through her Akashic studies evolved into direct messages—first for herself, then for humanity. These transmissions became the foundation for this book, *The Akashic Way*, a sacred offering for humanity's evolution and healing. She is now writing her second book, which explores the power of crises through the perspective of the Akashic Records, and continues to serve as a guide for seekers, artists, and changemakers drawn to purposeful living.

Along with her spiritual work, Mary has cultivated a celebrated career in film, television, and theater, which she continues to pursue today. She has earned three Emmy Awards and a Directors Guild of America Award for her direction on *General Hospital* (ABC), *Another World* (NBC), and NBC's Olympic Games. Her credits also span live news, sports, and talk shows for CBS, ABC, NBC, and MTV. Alongside directing film and theater, she is an accomplished screenwriter with multiple completed works and projects currently in pre-development.

Today, Mary's creative and spiritual callings live in collaboration. Whether writing, directing, or guiding someone through their Akashic Records, her mission remains the same: to bring Divine truth into human form—with clarity, grace, and a creative spark that uplifts the soul.

To connect with Mary and get more information visit:
https://theakashicway.com

www.ingramcontent.com/pod-product-compliance
Lightning Source LLC
Chambersburg PA
CBHW030920080726
47818CB00032BA/365/J